9 1.

1. c

John Huston: King Rebel

BY WILLIAM F. NOLAN

The Ray Bradbury Review—1952
Omnibus of Speed—1958
Adventure on Wheels—1959
Barney Oldfield—1961
Phil Hill: Yankee Champion—1962
Impact 20—1963
Men of Thunder—1964
When Engines Roar—1964
Man Against Tomorrow—1965
John Huston: King Rebel—1965
Sinners and Supermen—1965

BY WILLIAM F. NOLAN

JOHN HUSTON

KING REBEL

SHERBOURNE PRESS, INC.
LOS ANGELES, CALIFORNIA

First Printing

Copyright © 1965 by William F. Nolan

Library of Congress Catalog Card Number 65–15790

Acknowledgment is gratefully made to Universal-International for permission to use photos from *The List of Adrian Messenger* and to M-G-M/Seven Arts for permission to use photos from *The Night of the Iguana.*

To
Shelly
and
Anne,
who speak for Zorba

Acknowledgments

The author wishes to thank the following individuals—each of whom, in one way or another, contributed to the writing of this book.

Hollis Alpert
Eric Ambler
Eugene Archer
John Ardagh
Mary Astor
Lauren Bacall
Naomi Barry
Richard Basehart
Keyes Beech
Alfred Bester
Stephen Birmingham
Godfrey Blakeley
Barbara Browning
Art Buchwald
Richard Burton
Herb Caen
Truman Capote
Montgomery Clift
Mike Connelly

Opal Copley
Robert Coughlan
Bosley Crowther
Bette Davis
Olivia de Havilland
Dino De Laurentiis
Vittorio De Sica
Raymond Durgnat
William Eckhardt
Peter Ericsson
Allen Eyles
Jose Ferrer
Gerold Frank
Eugene Frenke
Zsa Zsa Gabor
Ava Gardner
Richard Gehman
Herbert Gold
James Goode

Ezra Goodman

Charles Grayson

Juliette Greco

Cynthia Grenier

Richard Griffith

Stephen Grimes

Evelyn Harvey

Sterling Hayden

Katherine Hepburn

Al Hine

Leonard Howard

Trevor Howard

Robert Hughes

Sam Jaffe

Charles Kaufman

Deborah Kerr

Laura Kerr

Evelyn Keyes

John Kilbracken

Arthur Knight

Dale Koby

Paul Kohner

Harry Kurnitz

Helen Lawrenson

Louis Linetsky

Anne Lowenkopf

Shelly Lowenkopf

Stephen Longstreet

Sue Lyon

Dwight Macdonald

David Mage

Cliff McCarty

Alice McIntyre

Burgess Meredith

Arthur Miller

Robert Mitchum

Audie Murphy

Stuart Palmer

Louella Parsons

Billy Pearson

Gregory Peck

Otto Preminger

Gottfried Reinhardt

Allen Rivkin

Mike Romanoff

Jaik Rosenstein

Lillian Ross

Froma Sand

Dore Schary

Philip K. Scheuer

George C. Scott

David Selznick

Mildred Simpson

Anthony Soma

Sam Spiegel

Ray Stark

Jerry Tallmer

Elizabeth Taylor

Thelda Victor

Peter Viertel

ACKNOWLEDGMENTS

Eli Wallach
John Wayne
Terry Wilson

Darryl F. Zanuck
Maurice Zolotow
Rose Zucker

with Special Thanks to RAY BRADBURY and, of course, to JOHN HUSTON and to all the others, unnamed . . .

William F. Nolan

Contents

John Huston: King Rebel

WHO (OR WHAT) IS JOHN HUSTON?

"To work with, he is unpredictable, inconsistent and volatile . . . a man who possesses real genius and is responsible for all that matters in every single department of every movie he directs. In his moments of inspiration, one stands aghast at his virtuosity. Yet . . . he makes errors of judgment, of taste, of understanding, so gross that one feels it cannot be the same man . . . Sometimes I despised him, hated him fiercely; sometimes I admired him beyond words . . . In Ireland his writers, actors, secretaries, technicians, backers, hangers-on—together with his friends, his wife and children, his horses and his dogs constitute the full Huston circus."

LORD KILBRACKEN

"John seems to destroy everything he loves."

GREGORY PECK

"He's a complete child of nature with no inhibitions . . . I'm still very fond of him . . . We simply spoiled a nice friendship by getting married."

                                                    EVELYN KEYES

"John was a very great love of mine . . . He needs the admiration of men as much as of women . . . He's capable of tremendous love of a very intense order . . . He's very sensitive . . . a man pursued by witches . . . and he broods about everything he's ever done wrong to anybody."

                                                    OLIVIA DE HAVILLAND

"Infinitely calm, inhumanly pleasant . . . he takes a quiet delight in tip-toeing along vertiginous emotional ravines with whatever notoriously high-strung people he has cajoled and charmed into coming with him . . . the kind of steaming, teeming, tense, nervous atmosphere in which he does his best work while everyone else goes to pieces."

                                                    HELEN LAWRENSON

"A natural-born antiauthoritarian individualistic libertarian anarchist, without portfolio . . . He is wonderful company, almost any time, for those who can stand the pace . . . One of the ranking grasshoppers of the Western Hemisphere . . . John was well into his twenties before anyone could imagine he would ever amount to more than an awfully nice guy to get drunk with . . . He operates largely by instinct, unencumbered by . . . any serious self-doubt. Incapable of boot-licking, he instantly catches fire in resistance to authority . . . His vocabulary ranges with the careless ease of a mountain goat between words of eight syllables and four letters . . . A rangy, leaping, thrusting kind of nervous vitality binds his pictures together."

                                                    JAMES AGEE

"His public style is composed of an impenetrable combination of calm good humor and rudely theatrical charm . . . In the world's remote and hostile regions he seems to travel with the immunity of a taboo figure whom it would be death to harm . . . In his denim bush jacket and velvet evening pumps encrusted with golden foxes he looks like an outsized portrait of Huckleberry Finn as painted by John Singer Sargent."

                                                    ALICE McINTYRE

"John collects people, odd people—bums, moochers, philosophical old drunks, talkative tarts—and jockeys like me . . . He doesn't seem to know any normal fears . . . and he has no concern for money . . . I've been around a lot of big spenders: Aly Khan, Nick the Greek, King Farouk—but they were amateurs compared to John. In Paris he'd give three thousand francs to a guy who handed him his binoculars . . . One day he said to me, 'Let's go skiing.' So we went out and bought a whole mess of ski equipment, the works, and took off . . . We got up to the top of this damned mountain, way the hell and gone up in the Sierras, so high it still makes me dizzy to think about it, and he turned to me and said: 'Now, what do we do, kid?' That's John for you!"

BILLY PEARSON

"A man of slow but sure intuition . . . he looks like a cross between an oil prospector and a beach attendant."

GODFREY BLAKELEY

"Dynamic, brilliant, amusing . . . Huston is a hare-brained madman . . . a laughing sadist who'd jab at your soul with an icepick . . . a shy, tender idealist, easily bruised, lonely, searching the world and himself to find out who he is . . . a hurricane of a man with an insatiable appetite for people, places and things . . . He is the first of Hollywood's creative artists, and the only one of the present generation to even approximate the measure of Eisenstein, Chaplin and D. W. Griffith . . . an impetuous daredevil who feeds upon the excitement of danger and the chase . . . He talks articulately and with relish in a warm, richly mellifluous voice . . . and his moods of enthusiasm, anger and ennui are overwhelming."

JAIK ROSENSTEIN

"One of the first of the hybrid writer-directors . . . a tough-minded nonconformist."

ROBERT COUGHLAN

"His character was clearly formed by the social forces predominant in the twenties, the disillusionment with large causes and the emphasis on experience for its own sake—violent action, boxing, travel, war—expressed in the spare, unadorned prose typical of the period . . . His visual style is unsurpassed among contemporary American directors."

EUGENE ARCHER

"When he looks through a camera lens he sees like nobody else in the world . . . He *paints* on celluloid."

JOSE FERRER

"John is really very forlorn, a very lonely man. He is out of touch with real human emotions."

GOTTFRIED REINHARDT

"Huston has the ability to take life without ducking . . . The world rushes on and most directors either go dead in the head or lose courage. Huston's got it in the head and his belly's full of courage."

VITTORIO DE SICA

"He is reckless . . . He has no respect for women. He uses them . . . and then ignores them. He is a mystery to himself, and he doesn't want to be analyzed."

TONY SOMA

"I just don't see how any woman could be around John Huston without falling in love with him."

MARILYN MONROE

"Mr. Huston is all *guy*, you know . . . a *guy's* guy."

TERRY WILSON

"He lives life the way many of us would like to but don't . . . John has left his friends' bodies strewn all over the world. When you are with him you have his undivided attention—until he feels the need to move on. Then there you are with egg on your face."

LAUREN BACALL

"John is one of the world's great romantics . . . with *grand luxe* tastes in food, clothes and women."

TRUMAN CAPOTE

"One of the most original characters in the whole world of cinema . . . vital, grandiose, cultivated, intelligent, mocking . . . Not even the legendary Powerscourt family in their heyday, with all their Cromwellian privileges, lived in a style approximating this modern Renaissance man . . . The John Huston Touch—you recognize it, you don't define it—is on every movie he makes."

NAOMI BARRY

"He is the Hamlet of American directors, in that he is still not sure of whether to be or not to be great . . . Perhaps his major flaw is that, like the inveterate gambler he is, he prefers to take on odds that are seldom in his favor."

HOLLIS ALPERT

"If a thing is easy, he's not interested. I wouldn't mind if he would only sweat once in a while. At least it would show he was human."

RICHARD BURTON

"He's a superb actor . . . and can show you so vividly what he wants you to achieve."

DEBORAH KERR

"He struts around Hollywood in a faun-green Donegal tweed suit with slash pockets, wearing a russet tweed cap . . . Not since Oscar Wilde lectured in a velvet cape carrying a lily, or Cecil B. DeMille donned puttees and swung a riding crop have we had as flamboyant a gentleman as John Huston."

HAZEL FLYNN

"He really is a character . . . and has been known to fly to remote movie locations with hundreds of pounds of excess wardrobe luggage. During one film, after almost six months of shooting, he had not worn the same outfit twice; he was always fastidiously and fantastically turned out in a different getup daily . . . He plays as hard as he works. Bogart and Huston once engaged in a football game at Huston's home in California, against movie executive Collier Young and another screen writer. The game was played in the mud, with a grapefruit, and everybody was in tuxedos. The spirit of competition became so keen that two of Young's ribs were fractured—and Ida Lupino, who had decided to get into the game, had her sacroiliac thrown out of joint."

EZRA GOODMAN

"Huston has more color than 90 per cent of the actors in Hollywood."

HUMPHREY BOGART

"Only seldom do you find a face like Huston's in an office. It's one that belongs on the road, in a boxcar doorway, in a mine, or in a Left Bank garret."

STERLING HAYDEN

"His thin, grooved face, brown as teakwood, looks Chinese . . . He's the last of the Regency bucks, elegant, extraordinary, unsentimental, uncompromisingly original . . . He can write his own ticket and thumb his nose at the tycoons."

ALFRED BESTER

JOHN HUSTON

"His career is curiously unequal . . . Often between the idea and the execution there interposes a kind of gangling, almost cynical nonchalance . . . John Huston is two people: the thoughtful, rather ascetic middlebrow, and the rugged extrovert for whom life is keenest during the brawl, the hunt and the drinking session."

RAYMOND DURGNAT

"Huston leaves most people a little dazed, no matter what experience they've gone through with him."

RICHARD GEHMAN

"Whatever *the* going thing is, John always goes with it."

STEPHEN GRIMES

"I don't believe that John will ever grow up—and I hope he doesn't."

LOUELLA PARSONS

"The guy will live forever. He's a hearty, tough soul. When he wants something from you, he sits down next to you and his voice gets husky, and pretty soon you're a dead pigeon."

DORE SCHARY

"He has a way of taking people apart, like a prosecuting attorney."

PAUL KOHNER

"Smooth-talking, hard-living . . . part hoodlum, part adventurer, part intellectual . . . a country squire (24 horses), hunter (stag, boar, fox), fisherman, global traveler, his style is Claridge's in London, the George Cinq in Paris, the St. Regis in New York."

JERRY TALLMER

"One of the most admired, rebellious and shadowy figures in the world of motion pictures."

LILLIAN ROSS

"He does not really live; he just plays the part of John Huston . . . and his entire life has been a magnificent performance."

MIKE ROMANOFF

Chapter 1

AN END AND A BEGINNING

Among the colorful restaurants of the world, Prince Mike Romanoff's in Beverly Hills has for many years meant something special to John Huston. It was here, after the war, that he'd proposed to actress Evelyn Keyes (who became his third wife—with the prince himself supplying the wedding ring) and, by 1950, many of the most pleasurably festive evenings of his life had been spent across a table at Mike's.

Therefore, on April 6 of that year, the date of his father's 66th birthday, Huston chose this restaurant in which to celebrate the event properly. Extensive preparations were made for a wild night of dining and drinking. As with all Huston parties, cost was ignored. (George Jessel once described Romanoff's as "the place where a man can take his family and have a lovely seven-course dinner for $3,400.")

An impressive group of friends had been invited to the affair, including Sam Spiegel, Jed Harris and Spencer Tracy. They would "take over" Romanoff's and provide Walter Huston with an evening to remember.

But following lunch that afternoon the veteran actor complained of stomach pains. "Afraid I can't make it over to Mike's tonight," he told his son.

John was concerned, yet without apparent cause. The elder Huston had just arrived in Hollywood to star in a new picture. Prior to his flight from New York he had been examined and pronounced in excellent health; perhaps this was simply an attack of indigestion.

"I'll get some rest and be fine by morning," Walter declared. "You go on without me."

Reluctantly, John went to the party. Without the guest of honor, the celebration rang hollow. Troubled, Huston returned early to the Beverly Hills Hotel; after looking in on his father he rented a room across the hall, feeling he should stay through the night.

John was awakened early the next morning. "The doctor says it looks like a blood clot," he was told. "It might be serious."

It was. At 8 A.M., with his son at his bedside, Walter Huston died of heart failure.

Pressed for comment, John slowly shook his head. "What the hell can you say? Except that Dad was too tough to get sick. He just *died,* that's all. He went fast, the way he wanted to go."

This statement seemed cold to some; they wanted Huston to talk about how great a talent his father was, about what "pals" the two had always been. They wanted Huston to say a lot more than he did. But he wouldn't.

He really didn't have to.

The relationship of Walter and John Huston had been obvious. Each had shared an abiding love and respect for the other; they had always been close. From the beginning. From the early days when young John roamed the country with his father, following the gaudy vaudeville circuits, living out of trunks, eating in cramped, dusty dressing rooms, traveling by night in weathered railroad coaches from one town to the next.

The beginning. . . . . . .

The family name was originally spelled Houghston, and John's great grandfather emigrated to the U.S. from Ireland in 1840. Four and a half decades later, in 1884, Walter was born in Toronto, Canada, of a Scotch mother (Elizabeth McGibbon) and an Irish father (Robert Houghston). It was decided that Walter should take up engineering—since his father was a successful contractor—and the boy did study along these lines for a time. However, from the moment of his initial exposure to dramatics (at the Toronto College of Music), young Walter was bent on acting. In 1902, at 18, he made his first stage appearance. Despite parental objections he joined a road company, which he accompanied to New York in 1905. That was the year he met Rhea Gore.

Rhea was a strong-willed newspaperwoman with a passion for travel and horses—but she was also home-minded when it came to marriage.

After Walter proposed, she agreed to become his wife on one condition. "You've got to settle down somewhere," she told him. "Acting is for gypsies and fools."

Huston was only 21; he could easily begin a new career. For Rhea's sake, he agreed to try.

They moved to Missouri where Walter became an engineer in charge of power and light for the small town of Nevada. (He later told John that his grandfather was a professional gambler, and that he'd originally won the town in a poker game. Young Huston never disputed this family legend.)

For an interim period Walter did well in his new profession, and the marriage seemed secure. On August 5, 1906, John Marcellus Huston was born. From the outset, Walter entertained his small son with vaudeville skits, and John's earliest memories are of his father's spirited singing and dancing each evening after dinner.

In an effort to increase his earnings, Walter signed up for a correspondence course, but his heart was not in engineering. He was apparently dreaming of Broadway one night when he turned off the water supply during a fire—and half the town burned down. By dawn the Hustons were headed for Weatherford, Texas.

St. Louis was next, and each time the family pulled up roots the marriage suffered. By 1909, having met a charming actress named Bayonne Whipple, Huston was itching for a return to the boards.

And when his employer told him that he would make a first-class engineer in another few years if he kept his nose to the grindstone Walter reacted in horror. He immediately exchanged grindstone for greasepaint and re-entered vaudeville. Bayonne went with him.

After the inevitable separation of his parents John Huston found himself shuffled from Walter to Rhea, and he grew up in many parts of the country.

At three and a half, he made his stage debut as Uncle Sam, replete in striped pants, string tie and tails. When the boy was seven his parents were divorced. Walter had officially teamed with Bayonne, as Whipple and Huston, and in 1914 she became his second wife.

"I traveled a great deal with each of my parents," John later stated. "From overnight fleabags with Dad to spacious hotels with Mother. She was crazy about playing the ponies, and I well remember a time when she was broke, down to 10 bucks. We were out at the track and she put the money on a 100-to-1 longshot that came in. She bought a fur coat, then played out the rest of the win at the track the next day. Lost every cent. We had to hock the coat to get home. She taught me that money's made for spending—and to hell with the odds!"

Huston's childhood was brutally realistic. His mother had no patience with myth and fantasy. John can still recall the Easter morning when she became annoyed with his search for colored eggs and told him: "Listen, I dyed those lousy eggs and hid them myself. There *is* no Easter Bunny."

With his father, it was the "three-a-day circuit," where the elder Huston often sang his own songs (*Why Bring That Up?* and *I Haven't Got the Do-Re-Mi*), alternating them with dramatic bits and soft shoe routines.

John was in and out of several schools by the time he was 12, when it was discovered that he had an enlarged heart complicated by a kidney ailment. The boy was placed in a private sanitarium where his life could be carefully supervised.

"They told me I was so delicate I might just die right there," Huston reports, "and that was when I began sneaking out at night to hit the waterfall."

The ritual of "hitting the waterfall" was the first major act of

rebellion associated with John Huston, and it chilled the blood of
the sanitarium staff when they discovered him at it. The frail youth
would strip off his pajamas, plunge into a stream which passed
through the grounds, and ride the swift current as it dropped
abruptly down over a steep waterfall.

"At first this scared the hell out of me," Huston recalls, "but I
instinctively realized that fear was a thing you *have* to conquer. I
conquered mine at that waterfall."

By 1918 John was in a California military school, but his illness
kept him from any real activity. Not until the following summer,
when he made his first trip to New York to visit his father, did
Huston's health show marked improvement.

Back in California, the boy attended Lincoln High in Los
Angeles, but quit at the end of his second year to become a boxer.
Over subsequent months, fighting as a lightweight, he won 23 of
25 bouts, breaking his nose in the process.

"The fact that boxing enabled me to travel up and down the
Pacific Coast had a lot to do with my going into it," he says. "I hated
staying put in one place—but after getting that broken beak it occurred to me that a kid as skinny as I was couldn't last much longer
in the racket."

Huston lasted long enough to wrap up the Amateur Lightweight
Boxing Championship of California. Then he headed east to celebrate his eighteenth birthday with his father in New York.

"That was a great summer," John says. "Rented a little apartment on MacDougal Street, a fourth floor walkup. Sam Jaffe had
the apartment above me, and he came down to ask me what I wanted
for my birthday. I told him a horse. Well, by God, if Sam didn't
go out and buy the oldest, saddest, most worn-out gray mare in New
York! Dad was starring on Broadway that year, and we all had a
hell of a wonderful time on my birthday."

Indeed, Walter Huston had come into his own as a top professional that season, winning high praise for his role in Eugene
O'Neill's *Desire Under the Elms*. After many lean years, he was
now established as an actor of dependability and solid talent.

His moody son was still seeking a place in life, and Walter
good-humoredly referred to John as "that wild Indian of mine."

Perhaps acting was the answer for young Huston's restlessness.

At least it seemed worth the gamble—and at 19 (aided by his
father's theatrical contacts) John landed a leading role in a Green-
wich Village production of Sherwood Anderson's *Triumph of the
Egg*. He followed this by appearing in Hatcher Hughes' *Ruint*, for
Kenneth MacGowan, with the Provincetown Players. (Sam Jaffe
was also in the cast.) Huston portrayed a rich young man who stops
off in a backwoods community, seduces a local belle, and is eventually run out of town on a rail. The play was not successful, and
John became disenchanted with acting.

"I was looking for adventure," he admits, "and I found it with
the Mexican cavalry."

Huston had been taking riding lessons from a German teacher,
Hattie Weldon, who was regularly visited by a general in the Mexican army. During one of these visits he watched young Huston
ride and offered him a commission with the cavalry, which the boy
happily accepted.

John's first marriage took place during this period "when I was
fresh out of my teens." The bride was a former high school sweet-
heart, Dorothy Harvey, and their union was short-lived. In Mexico,
Huston was again a bachelor.

"God, but those were great days," he says in recalling this stint
with the cavalry. "What a time we had! The Mexican officers drove
around in big Pierce-Arrows, drinking champagne. We'd make the
rounds, starting with a poker game in some big hacienda in the
morning. We'd take the game to a brothel, then finally to somebody's
hotel room where we'd play a kind of Mexican roulette. When some
guy won a big pot we'd turn out the lights, cock a loaded pistol
and throw it into the air. The pistol would go off when it hit the
ceiling. Then we'd turn the lights back on to see who was dead. If
the winner survived, he could keep the dough. If not, we all split
even."

Huston became a top jumping rider, and performed with the
troupe in a horse show at Madison Square Garden before resigning
his commission.

While in Mexico he'd written what he termed "a kind of musical play for puppets" which was staged by Ruth Squires in 1929 as
Frankie and Johnny (with Sam Jaffe composing and arranging the
score). When Boni and Liveright offered him a $500 advance against

a book publication of the play, the young author was stunned. Writing was suddenly more than a hobby; it paid off in solid cash! Instead of banking the check Huston took a train to Saratoga and promptly ran the publisher's advance up to $11,000 at the crap tables.

"But the story didn't end there," reports Huston. "I lost every cent before I left Saratoga. There were just too damn many crap tables."

Encouraged by this initial attempt at creative writing, Huston turned to fiction. His model was Ernest Hemingway, and he tried several short pieces in a similar stark, lean style, using what he knew about gambling, boxing and horses. Walter Huston showed one of these stories to Ring Lardner, who sent it along to H. L. Mencken at *The American Mercury*. It was bought, appearing in March of 1929 as *Fool*. Huston sent Mencken another called *Figures of Fighting Men*; it was also bought and printed.

That '29 season provided filmgoers with an opportunity to see Walter Huston in his first full-length feature, *Gentlemen of the Press*—and young John also made a brief screen appearance that same year with his father in a short entitled *Two Americans*.

"I even tried some opera singing around this time," admits Huston. "However, the less said about this the better."

In 1930 John's book was issued, brilliantly illustrated by the noted Mexican artist, Miguel Covarrubias. The publisher described it as "an adaptation for the stage of the song *Frankie and Johnny*, based on the many versions Mr. Huston has discovered throughout the country. Twenty of these appear at the back of the book, with a note on the St. Louis version, *Frankie and Albert*."

Huston still had no direction, no specific goal to pursue, but he felt that if he could write fiction and plays he could easily turn out professional news copy. After all, Hemingway began as a reporter.

John contacted his mother, who was then working for the New York *Graphic*, and she saw to it that her son got hired as a newspaperman. Huston's freewheeling, facts-be-damned approach enraged his employers.

"I was the world's lousiest reporter," he later admitted. "I'm sure that I was fired more times than any reporter in the paper's history. The city editor on nights hated my guts and he'd sack me at regular intervals—but the managing editor on days, a real nice fellow named Plummer, kept hiring me back."

Huston recalls the evening he impersonated a private detective during an assignment involving stolen jewels. A singer's pearl necklace had disappeared, and the woman agreed to put Huston on the case.

"I figured I could get a great story out of it," says Huston. "When I went to meet the gal at her club the cops were there, and I had to admit I was a reporter for the *Graphic*. But they didn't believe me. So I told them to call the city editor. Well, this was the same guy who kept firing me. They asked him if a reporter named Huston worked for the paper. 'Nope,' he said, 'I never heard of the son of a bitch.' Boy, that guy *really* hated my guts!"

John's last assignment on the paper marked his finish as a reporter; in writing up a Jersey crime story he switched the names of the victim and the accused. His discharge was permanent.

Back on the West Coast, Huston talked his way into a job as a contract writer with the Sam Goldwyn Studios at $150 per week. ("They were very impressed with anybody who'd published a book.") Yet no films came his way, and after six months of inactivity he walked out in disgust.

Walter Huston was by then a star at Universal, and his son joined him there on the promise of some script work. The promise was kept. John Huston received credit as "dialoguer" on an adaptation of Poe's *Murders in the Rue Morgue*, starring Bela Lugosi. He also helped write two films involving his father: *Law and Order*, an all-male western in which the elder Huston played a marshal named Frame Johnson who brings law and order to Tombstone by nearly killing everyone in town—and *A House Divided*, in which Walter essayed the role of a rugged New England fisherman who fights to keep the love of his mail-order bride. This was a William Wyler film, and young Huston was very impressed with Wyler's directorial talent.

Allen Rivkin, a veteran scribe at Warners who shared working quarters with Huston in 1931, has never forgotten him: "John would come pounding up the stairs of the writers' building to our second floor offices, his long legs loose and wobbly, his arms shooting in all directions, his head bobbing. I realized then why he had been such a successful boxer; his opponents never knew where to look for a blow!"

Rivkin continues: "One afternoon we all got stoned—I think we were celebrating not getting fired—John and I and another writer named Pinky Wolfson who was a real nut on weapons. Pinky owned a whole arsenal, and he had this vest-pocket .25 with him that day, showing off the gun to various secretaries. Well, John came to work dressed in a riding outfit, determined to show us how to take a thoroughbred mare over the jumps. For this demonstration he used the stairs, pretending they were obstacles on a jump course. So down he rode toward the first floor, drunk as sin, pounding his butt on the edge of the risers as he went, urging on his invisible horse.

"Now, Pinky had the .25 out and he was in the midst of some indoor target practice when one of the bullets hit a big globe hanging above the stairwell. Glass showered down over the steps in front of John, but that didn't stop him; he didn't even notice the broken glass. At the bottom, John stood up triumphantly, blood oozing from the seat of his ripped jodhpurs. He was an awful mess, and I rushed out for some iodine and bandages. When I got back with a first-aid kit John was missing. Seems he'd gone into Pinky's office to explain patiently to Wolfson the proper technique for firing a .25 indoors."

Now in his mid-twenties, Huston set out to see London, signing up to write for Gaumont-British films in England.

"When I got over there," he says, "I did damned little writing, but I got in a lot of bumming."

Huston found himself jobless and totally without funds thousands of miles from home. Out of pride, he refused to write his father for money. Instead, he sang on street corners in order to eat; at night he slept in Hyde Park, fighting for scraps of food with drunks and drifters.

"I managed to get over to Paris, where I spent the next year and a half as a starving artist," he says.

The French period was more "serious" than he likes to admit. Huston studied oil painting with an abiding passion; he found, in art, a clarity and order wholly lacking in his rootless existence. To help support himself, he sketched tourists at outdoor cafes, selling these sketches for wine and rolls. Thus, the world of art nurtured and absorbed him.

Legend has it that a beautiful young streetwalker from Montmartre provided John with his fare back to New York, but this has never been confirmed. Certainly the fabled Huston charm was much in evidence during these Paris days, and Huston *did* get back to New York—where he edited one of the town's first picture magazines, *The Mid-Week Pictorial.*

"That didn't last long," he relates, "so I headed for Chicago and another crack at acting."

John snared the lead in a WPA production of *Abe Lincoln in Illinois* (as adapted by Howard Koch) and considered the role something of a practical joke—since his father had won worldwide acclaim for a screen version of Lincoln in 1930, just three years earlier. During the play's run John met an attractive teen-aged Irish girl named Leslie Black. Within a half-hour after they'd been introduced he asked her to marry him; shocked, but amused, she said she'd think about it.

Over the next three years, keeping "on the bum" from city to city, Huston wrote a pair of unproduced plays: *Shadows Pursuing* (from a Hugh Walpole story) and *Storm Child* (in collaboration with R. F. Morris, Jr.). Despite the failure of these two ventures he was learning more about dialogue and about the craft of writing. By 1937 he had married Leslie Black and was headed for a career at Warner Brothers.

The wild years were by no means behind him, but now at least he had found a direction.

Chapter 2

BOGIE AND THE BLACK BIRD

John Huston's mother died in 1938, the same year that he became a contract writer at Warner Brothers—and his father had married for the third time (to Nan Sunderland). John was 32; he had already seen a lot of the world, and he was ready to stay put in Hollywood long enough to give his creative talent a chance to take root.

He worked on two films during that first season at Warners: *The Amazing Dr. Clitterhouse,* in which Edward G. Robinson portrayed a medical man who turns jewel thief in order to test his theories based on extensive criminal research—and *Jezebel,* the Bette Davis vehicle directed by William Wyler. *Clitterhouse* brought Huston and Humphrey Bogart (who was then 39) together professionally for the first time, and the two men began a close friendship which was binding until Bogart's death in 1957.

On *Jezebel,* Huston was lucky to have had Henry Blanke as associate producer, for it was Blanke who helped the younger man survive the cinema rat race. Huston might have bolted Hollywood without Blanke's steadying influence.

"I knew that Johnny had potential," Blanke later told an interviewer, "but when I first met him out here with his father he was just a drunken boy, hopelessly immature, without an ounce of discipline in his makeup. You'd see him at every party, a drink in his hand and a monkey on his shoulder. Marrying Leslie was probably the best thing that ever happened to him. She gave him standards to live by and the incentive to work."

During this era Warner Brothers excelled at making sociological gangster epics and in-depth film biographies, and Huston managed to co-write several of these, beginning with *Juarez* in 1939. Paul Muni starred in the title role, with Bette Davis as the Empress Carlotta and John Garfield as Porfirio Diaz. Huston collaborated with Wolfgang Reinhardt on this film—and when it was completed he felt confident enough to conduct a local workshop course in screen writing.

However, at the close of '39, Huston gave up teaching and left for New York to try his hand at directing a new Broadway play starring his father. John had never directed for stage or screen, but his natural enthusiasm and drive made up for any slight self-doubts, and he tackled the Broadway production of *A Passenger to Bali* with calm professional assurance.

Written by Ellis St. Joseph, most of the action took place aboard a freighter out of Shanghai, and concerned the evil doings of a phony man of the cloth, the Reverend Mr. Walkes (Walter Huston), who incited the crew to mutiny and led the ship's captain to the brink of murder. Walkes was finally left to go down with the sinking ship during a typhoon.

In staging this drama at the Ethel Barrymore Theater John conjured up a very effective typhoon sequence and elicited a gusty performance from his father, but these virtues were not sufficient to keep the play afloat. It sank (on March 16, 1940) after only four performances, and the Hustons returned to Hollywood.

John's next writing assignment for Warners was another film biography, *Dr. Ehrlich's Magic Bullet,* again with Robinson (as the man who discovered a cure for syphilis). The screenplay was solid enough to win an Academy Award nomination in 1940.

Huston hated to work in the morning—and he made it routine not to arrive at the studio until after lunch, thus drawing sharp criticism from several members of the studio's high brass. Only the intervention of Blanke and a few other supporters saved his job. As one awed fellow-writer observed: "Huston's flag of vociferous independence flies high over a community where the Big Fear prevails."

After he helped write another Academy Award nominated script (*Sergeant York*), the nabobs at Warners realized that they couldn't afford to lose John Huston. The moment talent pays off in Hollywood eccentricities are forgiven—and instead of being fired Huston was given a raise and asked to apply his skills to the job of turning W. R. Burnett's crime novel, *High Sierra*, into a workable film script.

This gangster epic proved a turning point in the careers of both Bogart and Huston. In Bogie's case it was his first really important role, elevating him to star status. ("I'd always been the guy behind the guy behind the gun!") It led John Huston into the final major phase of his professional life—as a film director.

"They promised me that if I did the right kind of job in adapting *Sierra* they'd let me direct my next one," says Huston.

This picture told the story of a hunted criminal (Bogart) who flees on foot into the Sierra Madres toting his machine gun in a violin case. He is surrounded by police and fatally wounded in a violent gun battle, dying as "the last of the gangsters."

Raoul Walsh, who directed *High Sierra*, revealed that George Raft was the studio's original choice for the role, "but this time Raft refused to die on screen, so we got Bogie. He didn't mind getting shot by the cops."

Huston collaborated with Burnett on the final script, which won studio approval. Now Huston had a go-ahead as director if and when he could find the right property.

Someone suggested a remake of Dashiell Hammett's *The Maltese Falcon*, and Huston liked the idea. Even though the book had been filmed twice before by Warners, John was convinced that it had never been properly done and that it would lend itself to a stark, gritty treatment in line with Hammett's style. Warners had released the first version in 1931 under the original title, starring Ricardo Cortez as detective Sam Spade and Bebe Daniels as the double-crossing girl. Roy del Ruth directed with a heavy accent on comedy and the picture failed to come off. Warner's tried again in 1936, changing the plot completely; this time the story involved a mythical horn filled with gems in place of the falcon. The directorial reins were turned over to William Dieterle. Warren William played the detective, and Bette Davis essayed the girl. It ran through several titles from *Men on Her Mind* to *Hard Luck Dame,* but emerged as *Satan Met A Lady.* Brown Holmes, one of the original scripters in '31, did the solo screenplay—and the approach was, to quote one critic, "nonsensical." It fizzled at the box office.

"I knew that if I could get a solid screenplay out of the book they'd let me direct it," says Huston. "Then the damndest thing happened!"

It seems that Huston gave the book to his secretary and told her to recopy the printed text, breaking it down into shots, scenes and dialogue. A copy of this fell into the hands of Jack Warner, and he thought that Huston had adapted the Hammett story into a final screenplay. "I just read it and it's *great,*" Warner told him. "You've really captured the flavor of this book. Now go shoot it with my blessings."

Huston was stunned and delighted.

He naturally intended making some changes in the script, but for the moment all was well.

Casting, however, was a problem. Who would play Sam Spade?

Raft was pegged for the role, but refused it, and once more Bogart stepped into the breach. Bogie's approach was tough, slightly sadistic, cunning, unsentimental and brutally honest. He *was* Spade.

For the pivotal role of Gutman, the Fat Man, Huston signed up Sydney Greenstreet, a 61-year-old, 285-pound stage actor. Greenstreet had been playing comedy parts on Broadway for three decades, and was acting Shakespeare as early as 1904, yet had never made a motion picture. Huston saw him as the ideal Gutman.

For Hammett's scheming, lying Brigid O'Shaughnessy, Huston chose Mary Astor, who projected just the proper blend of sensuality and false innocence. Peter Lorre made a wonderfully whining Joel Cairo, and Elisha Cook was extremely effective as Wilmer, the trigger-tense killer who worked for the Fat Man.

Walter Huston was set to appear in a "bit"—as bloody, bullet-riddled Captain Jacobi, who staggers into Spade's office to die clutching the falcon. ("Dad said he wanted to appear in every film I directed, for luck.")

Hal Wallis was producer, with Henry Blanke as his associate. Blanke agreed to work closely with Huston. His advice to the neophyte director: "Shoot each scene as though it is *the* most important one in the picture. Make every shot count. Nothing can be overlooked, no detail ignored."

Huston took Blanke's advice—and prepared literally hundreds of sketches, demonstrating precise camera angles, set construction and cast positions. His art study in Paris was now paying dividends.

The plot revolved around a group of bizarre characters desperately intent on tracking down a jewel-encrusted statuette of a black bird. The girl Brigid attempts to use Sam Spade to help gain sole possession of the bird, leading him on with conflicting stories through three murders. Their eventual encounter with the Fat Man, who takes possession of the falcon only to find it a clever fake, leads to the climax in which Sam discovers it was Brigid who actually murdered his business partner. She pleads for release, telling Spade she loves him—but the detective coolly turns her in with the dry comment: "I'll wait for you, angel. Unless they hang you. Then I'll always remember you."

Completed in two months, at a cost of less than $300,000, this film set the pattern for a host of imitations—but the Huston/Hammett combination was never equalled. From first scene to last, *The Maltese Falcon* achieved tremendous force and drive, due in large part to Huston's imaginative, meticulous direction. He insisted, for example, that Mary Astor run around the set several times before she appeared on camera to give her a certain nervous, quick-breathing appeal. He shot up at Greenstreet from low angles, emphasizing the immense bulk of this character; he used a deep-focus lens to establish group tensions—and his sets had the seedy, lived-in atmosphere of reality, heightened by harsh lighting which did nothing to "soften" the action.

Walter Huston was proud of his son's work, and even admitted to being a trifle nervous about his single cameo scene as the expiring Jacobi. This gave John an idea, and when his father had finished the scene and was back in his apartment the phone rang. The caller said she was the producer's secretary and that Mr. Wallis had seen the rushes and felt that Walter had "over acted" in knock-ing down a lamp in the course of his death bit. Would he mind coming back to the studio for a retake? Huston, shaking with anger, stated that he had *never* been accused of overacting, but that he'd be in the next morning to redo the scene. Then a man's voice cut in: "Walter, this is Wallis. Hope you don't mind a retake. You were pretty *bad,* you know."

Huston almost dropped the phone in his rage. "Goddammit, I *said* I'd do the fool scene again, didn't I?" The man on the other end of the line roared with laughter—and only then did Huston discover that his son was "Hal Wallis" and that Mary Astor had been drafted into impersonating the secretary.

John ribbed his father about this for years.

A minor furor erupted regarding the film's title: Warners wanted to call it *The Gent from Frisco,* since they had already used the original title in '31, but Huston stood firm and the substitution was dropped.

When *Falcon* was released, in October of 1941, the critics im-mediately dubbed it "a classic in its field," and Britain's *Films and Filming* later selected it for their *"Great Films of the Century"* series, stating: "The picture is more compact and unified than the novel, and Huston has made precise deletions. The narrative is considerably tightened . . . Huston displays a rare talent for the film medium in his exact manipulation of actors, cameramen, set designers and others, to capture such a rich, near flawlessly correct mood throughout the length of the film . . . Continually the director enlarges our under-standing . . . It is finally a study of people affected by the weakness of greed, realized with a force and a psychological aptness that gives it moral purpose . . . and more than just a private-eye picture, this is a compelling study in human frailty."

Critic James Agee termed it simply "the best private-eye melo-drama ever made," and it was nominated for an Academy Award as Best Picture of 1941.

The box-office was so strong on this initial Huston effort that Warners announced that a sequel would soon follow: *The Further Adventures of the Maltese Falcon* to be written and directed by Huston, re-teaming Bogart, Astor, Greenstreet and Lorre. However, this project apparently never got beyond the publicity stage. By December the fast-moving Huston was back in Manhattan with his vital new play (co-authored by Howard Koch), *In Time to Come*.

Produced by Otto Preminger, the play dealt with Woodrow Wilson's fight for the League of Nations at the end of World War I. Not a popular success, closing after 40 Broadway performances in late January of 1942, it nevertheless won the coveted New York Drama Critics Circle Award that season, edging out John Steinbeck's *The Moon Is Down*.

Huston was now the talk of the film capital, and when he returned to the Coast in '42 Howard Koch went with him to write the screenplay for John's second directorial effort, *In This Our Life*, starring Bette Davis, Olivia de Havilland, George Brent and Dennis Morgan, based on Ellen Glasgow's novel about a decaying Southern family. This story was, as Huston later commented, "pretty heavy going." Basically a romantic melodrama involving the loves of two sisters, the final product emerged as workmanlike but undistinguished.

Across the Pacific, completed that same year, was much more to Huston's liking, and his *Falcon* cast (Bogart, Astor and Greenstreet) turned in excellent performances. With a screenplay by Richard Macaulay, based on a *Post* serial by Robert Carson, the film cast Greenstreet as an urbane spy for the Japanese, who is defeated in an attempt to blow up the Panama Canal by Bogie in true comic-strip tradition. The wartime plot was weak, but Huston managed to inject an impressive amount of atmospheric detail and characterization into what might otherwise have emerged as a hack thriller.

The wildly-improbable ending was not actually directed by Huston, since real war intervened to take him away from this artificial celluloid conflict. Earlier in '42 he was commissioned in the U.S. Army Signal Corps (as a lieutenant) and his duty papers arrived when he was winding up the Bogart film.

As Huston told the story to writer Jerry Tallmer: "A small package had come to me in the mail. I didn't look at it too closely, and put it aside, not realizing that the package contained my shipping orders. Then I got this phone call from some major in Washington asking me why the devil I hadn't reported. I told him that it was a mistake, and that I only needed a few more days to finish my picture, but he wouldn't listen. He gave me just 24 hours to report.

"I sat right down and altered the script and set up a wild scene with Bogie trapped in Panama. Made him a prisoner of the Japanese who were out to bomb the Canal. I fixed it so his hands were tied behind him and packed the room with Japanese soldiers armed with machine guns. Outside, more armed soldiers surrounded the house.

"That night we shot it right up to the part where Bogie is hopelessly trapped. I knew there was no way in God's green world he could logically have escaped. I also knew Warners would never re-shoot the whole ending. I had them. So I waved goodbye to Bogie—and was in Washington the next morning."

Director Vincent Sherman inherited the unenviable job of getting Bogart out of Huston's trap—and shooting was called off for two days while the baffled director and a squad of writers attempted to solve the dilemma. As finally filmed, a Japanese soldier suddenly goes mad and begins shooting up the room; Bogart comes out of the melee with a gun in his fist, boasting, "I'm not easily trapped." Sherman sighed when the scene's logic was questioned. "Listen, if you ask me, we were lucky to get the bastard out of there at all!"

Warners forgave Huston, and while he was back in Hollywood awaiting overseas orders they allowed him to work on the script of *Background to Danger* for George Raft. Huston was not happy about having to shelve plans for *Moby Dick* (in which his father would star as Captain Ahab) but agreed to sit in on story conferences involving the Raft project.

According to Ezra Goodman, Huston was attending one of these story confabs that summer "sitting there in his uniform with his long legs propped up on the desk, cap pushed back on his head, sketching and listening . . . Finally he stood up, yawned, pulled down his cap and said, 'Sorry, gentlemen, but I have a date in the Aleutians.' Then he walked out."

In August of 1943 the U.S. Signal Corps released a stark, stunning documentary: *Report From the Aleutians.*

John Huston had gone to war.

Chapter 3

A CLOSE-UP LENS ON COURAGE

During the late summer of 1942 Huston and his six-man camera crew accompanied a U.S. task force to the barren Pacific Island of Adak at the tip of the Aleutians. These islands were then the take-off point for American attacks against enemy-held Attu and Kiska. On Adak, where most of Huston's first documentary was shot, a tidal flat had been converted into a runway for Liberator bombers.

Very little was known about this area, and Huston remained on the remote atoll for six months in order to document fully the tough Aleutian struggle. Bad weather was constant, and John's color camera followed the wind-whipped bulldozers as they fought through impossible terrain in the massive effort to establish a functional base on Adak.

In the course of 15 attack trips into Japanese territory, Huston and his men rode the big bombers through fiery curtains of exploding flak over heavily-guarded Kiska, recording each raid—and narrowly escaping disaster in a crash landing.

John had his second brush with death when a 20 mm shell from a diving Zero killed the young waist gunner next to him. ("That kid died and I lived—and who knows why?")

When his 47-minute documentary was released, with Walter Huston delivering the spoken narration, the New York *Times* called it "one of the most remarkable pictorial records to emerge from this war."

As a result of *Report From the Aleutians*, Huston was promoted to captain—and sent to England on another assignment.

"It seems that President Roosevelt had asked to see a film on the North African Allied task force landings," relates Huston. "And there *wasn't* any. So they flew me over to England to help make one. It was to be a Joint Operation film, under the supervision of Frank Capra, but the whole thing fizzled. The English had some swell footage. Yet the only American footage on the fighting in North Africa had gone down with a boat and been lost—so we were forced to *fabricate* combat film out in California and Florida. There were canvas tanks and glorious air battles over Orlando, and the War Department was satisfied. After a long while the film was edited and put together, but that was the extent of it. The mess was never released, which was a blessing."

In England, Huston encountered Eric Ambler, and he invited the novelist to join his crew "just for the sport of it." Ambler, then with the British forces, wrangled permission—and they all took off for southern Italy, where Huston was to make a documentary showing the hardships of the Italian campaign. Lieutenant Jules Buck, in charge of the camera crew, revealed that the "script" for what was eventually called *The Battle of San Pietro* was handwritten by Huston each night after a day in the field. Between lulls in the fighting he would re-shape it as events dictated. The footage was processed in Washington, and there were no "rushes" to correct or examine.

"We couldn't really plan ahead too much," Buck says, "because we'd sometimes get pinned down behind a hedgerow for half a day, ducking what the Nazis threw at us."

The small 700-year-old hillside village of San Pietro, heavily fortified by the Germans, was the key to the Liri Valley, down which ran the road to Rome. In that vital winter of 1943 this mountain town had to be captured by Fifth Army troops in order to insure the success of the entire Italian campaign.

"We were in on the start of things there," says Huston. "Our unit followed a Texas infantry regiment, the 143rd of the 36th Division, all the way through the fighting. The courage of these men was fantastic. I've never seen anything to match it."

An Army Intelligence error almost wiped out Huston and his small crew. "We were informed that the Germans had pulled back, out of San Pietro, and that it was okay to advance," relates Huston. "Jules and Eric and I cut across the fields toward the village. We were well ahead of the troops and wanted to get some street footage. I was limping—had sprained an ankle—and this slowed us up. Saved our lives, in fact, because when we reached the wall at the base of the hill leading up to the village the Germans lobbed in a couple of mortar shells. In the dust these raised we got out okay, but I was annoyed as hell over the mistake."

This may well have occasioned the incident which James Agee later related: "Once, while he was in Italy, John sprinted up five flights of headquarters stairs in order to sock a superior officer. Arriving at the top, he was so winded he could hardly stand. Time enough to catch his breath was time enough to cool off; he just wobbled downstairs again."

A series of bitter, brutal attacks was launched against the occupied town, despite the fact that the Nazi forces put up a murderous wall of fire against the advancing infantrymen. In the crippling cold of an Italian winter the battle for San Pietro was waged—and Huston got it all on film, weaving through the hills and orchards, lying in foxholes as the earth shuddered under the bombs of diving Stukas, pinned down by crossfire as he ranged ahead of the American troops—moving continually from one of his crew to the next, showing them exactly what shots he wanted. Some members of his crew lost up to 30 pounds in weight.

As Herbert Gold put it in a no-nonsense program note for the film: "John Huston and the others were there, no shit, really right there under fire while the men were dying. Their hand-held cameras went whirling in the violence, courage and desperation of mortal events, and the faces of the cameramen were brother to the faces of the men who lay broken-skulled and destroyed."

Eleven hundred replacements were fed into the regiment after San Pietro. It was a literal blood bath.

This marked the first time that real in-the-field combat, involving Americans, had ever been seen on the screen. Agee wrote: "Time and again Huston was spared an arm or a leg only by the grace of God and the horrified vigilance of his friend, Jules Buck. John would saunter through mine fields oblivious of danger, the beau ideal of the contrivers of booby traps."

The filmed result was savage and wholly uncompromising, a painfully true testament to the horrors of war. Scenes of survivors grimly gathering the dead in white bag-shrouds, of wounded and dying American soldiers writhing on the cold earth, of entire patrols being cut down by shell-fire—all these formed too strong a dose for the War Department. The print was cut from five reels to three: it was "softened" for home consumption—and a Mormon Choir was dubbed in on the soundtrack. But what remained, even in its edited form, exceeded in scope and realism anything that had been done in the way of a wartime documentary.

"We finally got into the village after the Germans had withdrawn," says Huston, "and the villagers themselves came slowly out of hiding, from caves and basements, mostly old people and kids. That's when we got the stuff with the kids."

This sequence, ending the film, reveals the numbed, death-stamped faces of the children of San Pietro, while Huston's calm, softly spoken narration states that in a few years "they'll have forgotten there ever was a war." Its irony was deliberate, for it was obvious that these mute, broken children would never forget what they had seen here.

Time magazine called Huston's film "the most humane, most moving, most nearly perfect of our documentaries—it achieves pure tragic grandeur." And the *Nation* commented: "It is clear that Huston understood what he was recording and how to record it, with a wonderfully vigorous and whole maturity, at once as a soldier, an artist and a man."

A British critic wrote: "It is . . . the finest film to come out of World War II. The raw, gray photography captures the poverty and ugliness of this environment without neglecting the stark, elemental beauty of the mountains . . . here is as solemn a protest against warfare as the screen has ever depicted."

The released print ran just 32 minutes, and featured a Preface to the action, spoken by General Mark Clark.

"The War Department chose him," says Huston. "They wanted Clark to say something that would take about three minutes on the screen, so I wrote a kind of model, explaining the purpose of the Italian campaign and so on, figuring that Clark would naturally have it redone by his staff at the Pentagon. But he memorized the whole damn speech! Now, here was this four-star general repeating, word for word, the strategy of the campaign as I saw it . . . and me just a dogface in it! I guess he didn't know anymore about what was going on than I did."

When Huston returned from Italy, in February of 1944, he had been promoted to the rank of major, and was awarded the Legion of Merit for his outstanding work in the field. With Jules Buck he edited *San Pietro* in the summer of '44, but Army brass held up the film's release, fearing its anti-war effect on possible enlistees. (Huston was amused, some years later, to find a drastically-edited version being used to help recruit new soldiers. "All of the blood and death had been carefully removed.")

That March, during a newspaper interview in Alaska, Olivia de Havilland declared her "deep love" for Huston, adding: "I am ready to marry John whenever he is free."

Huston's marriage to Leslie Black had been in trouble for quite some time, and Miss de Havilland's statement was no publicity stunt. (Many years later she told a reporter: "John fell in love with me and pursued me relentlessly. I ran away from him on several occasions. Once he drove all night to find me in Carmel, abandoning a film to go after me.")

By April of 1945, when *San Pietro* was finally released, Huston was in Las Vegas, obtaining a divorce from his second wife. He attended a cocktail party at producer David O. Selznick's home in Beverly Hills that same month. In a mood of depression, he began drinking steadily. Quick to take offense at a casual remark made by Errol Flynn, Huston sullenly invited the hard-muscled actor out to the garden. Flynn accepted.

"That fight was a honey," said one witness. "Errol knocked John down 10 times!"

At the tenth knockdown, standing over Huston, Errol threw up his hands: "Jeez, Johnny, don't get up again! Let's just quit."

"That's when I knew I had him," the battered Huston was quoted as saying.

Huston's third and final Army documentary was never seen by the public. Entitled *Let There Be Light*, it was filmed entirely at the Mason General Hospital on Long Island, and commissioned by the War Department.

"They told me they wanted a film to show to industry, to prove that nervous and emotional veterans were not lunatics," says Huston. "At that time these men just weren't getting jobs. Our purpose was to help them."

It was necessary to obtain footage on actual interviews and psychiatric treatment at the hospital. Huston set up several hidden cameras to record the emotionally disturbed veterans as they discussed their problems and, later, as they were put under hypnosis and given drugs and medicine. No written script was used; each foot of film was genuine, unplanned. (Later Huston added the narration, which his father read onto the soundtrack.)

"This was the most joyous, hopeful thing I ever had a hand in," says Huston. "I felt as though I were going to church every day I went out there to that hospital."

At one point in the film a young soldier, who had developed a terrible stutter in battle due to the hiss of high-explosive shells, suddenly found that he had regained the power of clear speech: "I can talk, I can talk! Listen, I can talk! Oh God, Listen! I can talk!"

To get moments such as this, Huston often had three cameras operating at once, but he repeatedly declared: "I take no credit for this. What happened there in front of us was a wonder and a miracle."

The *Nation* called *Let There Be Light* "noble and fiercely moving," and film critic Archer Winston said (in the New York *Post*): "It's so great a picture, so inspiring medically and humanly, so tremendously graphic . . . of basic fears and joy . . . that seeing it I felt as if I had never before witnessed emotion on the screen so stripped of self-consciousness . . . it is a visible ascent from Hell . . . an experience to remember for years."

When the War Department restricted the film, refusing to release it, Huston was shocked and outraged.

"I never dreamed they'd ban it," he said. "I guess they didn't want the public to see what war can do to a man's emotions and nerves—so they claimed that it would be an invasion of privacy to let the film be shown. Yet we had obtained signed releases from each of the patients.

"Years later, some friends of mine who wanted very much to see this film asked me to arrange a showing at the Museum of Modern Art in New York. So I did. The Army Public Relations Office gave me their okay to screen it. Well, just before it was shown, minutes before, a bunch of MPs arrived and seized the print and took it right back to Washington. The PRO people had reversed their decision."

Let There Be Light was never taken off the restricted list, notwithstanding the concerted efforts of Huston and several influential critics and film notables. In 1947 a re-make called *Shades of Gray* was produced as a "commercial" version of the original in which the psychoneurotic veterans were replaced by professional actors.

As John Huston sadly remarked: "It was hardly the same thing."

Chapter 4

OF LOVE AND EXISTENTIALISM

Just prior to his enlistment Huston had completed the final polishing on an original screenplay (written with Howard Koch) called *Three Strangers*. Huston had conceived it with Bogart, Greenstreet and Mary Astor in mind early in 1942, and the plot was in the mold of *The Maltese Falcon*. It dealt with a mystery woman who picks up two men on the eve of the Chinese New Year and takes them to her apartment, telling them that the Goddess Kwan Yin will grant the wish of any three strangers who make a combined prayer to her on this particular night. Their wish is granted, and leads to tragedy.

When the film was produced for Warners by Wolfgang Reinhardt in 1945 he chose Jean Negulesco to direct (as Huston was occupied elsewhere), and got Greenstreet and Lorre for the two male leads, with Geraldine Fitzgerald playing the mystery girl. The "three strangers" wish for money, and indeed a Grand National Sweepstakes ticket held by Lorre comes in at 30,000 pounds.

In the climax, Greenstreet uses a statuette of the Goddess to club Miss Fitzgerald to death, then turns himself in to the police. Lorre is left holding a ticket he cannot redeem, since to do so would involve him in murder. The film ends on this note of irony—and the theme of unattainable riches which Huston had first pursued with *Falcon* was repeated here.

When *Three Strangers* was completed Huston was on a screen version of Ernest Hemingway's *The Killers* for Mark Hellinger, but he never received any official credit for his first-draft screenplay. Hemingway is reported to have considered it the finest adaptation he had yet seen on his work, and since the two writers were very close in spirit and philosophy this is not surprising. (The credit on *The Killers* finally went to Anthony Veiller, who was later to become Huston's chief script collaborator.)

Out of the service, and once again a bachelor, Huston was characteristically active on the woman front. In late June of 1946 he met the fetching young blonde actress Evelyn Keyes, and was immediately attracted to her. ("We'd both been married twice so that gave us something in common!")

Miss Keyes, then in her twenties, had been a friend of John's father for several years, and had accompanied the elder Huston on a bond-selling tour during the war. "Walter was *so* proud of his boy. He kept dragging out pictures of John and talking about him," she said. "My curiosity was aroused. We eventually met at a party, leaving early arm in arm. John was the most direct, vital man I'd ever encountered."

Huston proved just *how* direct he could be when he leaned across a table at Romanoff's that July and asked Evelyn to marry him.

"When?" she asked him.

"Right now, tonight," he told her.

She said yes—and that word set things in wild motion. Mike Romanoff rushed home to get a wedding band a guest had lost in his swimming pool, while Huston phoned pilot Paul Mantz and chartered a private plane to fly them to Nevada. At 3:30 A.M. they were pounding on the door of Gene Ward, a local Justice of the

Peace in Las Vegas. With Mantz and a taxi driver as witnesses they were married that same morning.

Huston took his new bride out to his personally-designed California ranch in Tarzana. It featured oiled-pine outer walls, high ceilings and a diving board on the upstairs porch overlooking the pool. The high ceilings had provoked a disgruntled comment from Frank Lloyd Wright when he'd stopped by to inspect the house.

"Wright told me he never would have designed the place that way," Huston relates. "Told me that low ceilings lend a sense of security and warmth to a house, but I explained to him that I stood well over six feet and just couldn't risk bumping my head. Mr. Wright, of course, was a much smaller man. I remember he gave me a long, sour look and said, 'Anyone over five ten is a weed!' Then he put on his hat and walked out."

Existentialism was an unfamiliar term to Americans in 1946. Frenchman Jean-Paul Sartre was the chief prophet of this new form of atheistic belief which stated that "man is responsible only to himself in a world devoid of purpose spinning in a meaningless universe." This philosophy was causing intense excitement in Paris, and Sartre had written a play incorporating it called *Huis-Clos*. In London, when Alec Guinness had starred, the play was entitled *Vicious Circle*. Now, as *No Exit*, it was scheduled for a Broadway production at the Biltmore Theater—with John Huston directing.

The setting is a single room in Hell, and the three main characters are Cradeau (Claude Dauphin), a sadistic, cowardly collaborator, Inez (Annabella), an embittered lesbian—and Estelle (Ruth Ford), a nymphomaniac who has murdered her illegitimate child. They are to spend eternity together in this single, stark room, verbally ripping away at one another.

For Huston, directing this hour-long stage vehicle represented a special challenge. He would have to work close to his characters, moving them to create tension and personal friction, since direction means everything to a one-set production such as this. Additionally, Existentialism was a controversial concept, with Huston, in effect, introducing it to the U.S.

In a wave of word-of-mouth publicity, *No Exit* opened on November 26, 1946—but the play never caught fire with the ticket-buying public. Those who saw it appreciated the flourish and skill with which it was done, but the production had to close down a few days before Christmas, after a total of just 31 performances.

The majority of critics, however, had been completely won over. "Presented with a kind of ruthless intellectual passion . . . under John Huston's revealing direction," said *Theatre Arts*—and John Mason Brown, in the *Saturday Review,* found the play ". . . sensitively and unflinchingly directed by Huston." *Time* called it "a piece of bold, unusual theater. . . . The characters seem like arch-symbols of the disordered age from which so stark a philosophy emerged."

No Exit won the New York Drama Critics Circle Award as the best foreign play of the year—and Huston was able to claim a critical success.

He left New York for California, brimming with plans for the biggest gamble of his career, a film he would shoot in Mexico from a novel he had long wanted to direct, *The Treasure of the Sierra Madre.*

Chapter 5

OSCAR HUNTING IN MEXICO

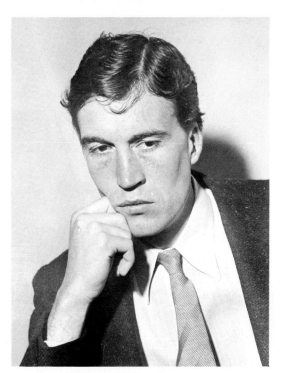

Young John (shown with his father, Walter Huston)
during the early Thirties, when he was co-writing such
screenplays as A House Divided and Law And Order.

A scene from the first feature Huston directed,
THE MALTESE FALCON, featuring Sydney Greenstreet
and Humphrey Bogart.

John and his third wife,
Evelyn Keys, after their
marriage in 1946.

The Academy Award winning team on the set of
THE TREASURE OF THE SIERRA MADRE.

Bogie and Bacall, the stars of KEY LARGO,
on location with Huston.

Made up for a bit part
(later cut out) in his own
film with star
Audie Murphy.

The director sprays
Royal Dano (as The
Tattered Soldier) in
THE RED BADGE OF
COURAGE.

Huston directs
Jose Ferrer (as the
dwarfish
Toulouse-Lautrec)
on the set of
MOULIN ROUGE
in Paris.

In fringed buckskin jacket, Huston poses at
sea with MOBY DICK star Richard Basehart.

In Japan, for THE BARBARIAN AND THE GEISHA,
Huston calms a disturbed John Wayne.

The director muses, conjuring up fresh problems for his cast and crew.

Faces of experience: Huston and Gable, on THE MISFITS.

First published in the mid-thirties, *The Treasure of the Sierra Madre* was written by the mysterious B. Traven, who shied away from publicity, avoided photographers and interviewers, and cut himself off from all public contact by living alone in the depths of Mexico. No one in Hollywood had ever seen the man, but Huston had been able to make contact through the author's literary agent. He had exchanged letters with Traven occasionally during the war, but it was not until 1946 that Huston wrote to inform the novelist that a definite shooting schedule had finally been set for *Treasure*.

"I'd been itching to make this for years," says Huston. "Warners bought it before the war, and a couple of times while I was overseas they almost put it into production. But Henry Blanke held the property for me."

Traven sent Huston a reply which ran 20 pages, filled with suggestions regarding filming, lighting and set construction. This letter inspired Huston to ask for a personal interview. "I can guarantee nothing," Traven wrote back, "but if you will come to the Hotel Reforma in Mexico City, early in January, I will try and meet you there. I make no promises."

Huston decided to take a chance, and headed for Mexico City on the date Traven had specified. He waited patiently at the Reforma, but the mystery man did not appear. After several days of frustrating silence Huston was preparing to leave when he was handed a card bearing the words: "H. Croves—Translator—Acapulco."

"A thin little guy with gray hair, dressed in faded khaki, stepped up to me," relates Huston. "Showed me a typed note from Traven which said 'This man knows my work better than I do.' Then he told me that Mr. Traven couldn't make it, but that he was authorized to answer any and all questions I might wish to ask."

Huston ended up hiring Croves as a technical advisor for location shooting in Mexico (at a salary of $150 per week). He and his art director, John Hughes, had made an 8,000 mile scouting trip over Mexico to pick out the proper site, and they had chosen the rugged, mountainous country surrounding the small village of Jungapeo, near San Jose de Purua.

Having become accustomed to the rigors (and advantages) of location filming as a result of his wartime documentaries, Huston insisted that the studio allow him and his crew at least two months in Mexico on *Treasure*. In 1947 this was a revolutionary request, and Henry Blanke had to personally convince Jack Warner that such a plan was feasible. Reluctantly, Warner agreed to finance the expedition with Blanke as producer.

Traven's novel (as adapted by Huston) concerned itself with three men who go into the Sierra Madres in frenzied search of treasure: Dobbs, a brute whose moral code is nonexistent; Curtain, a raw youth whose life is yet to be shaped; and Old Howard, a veteran prospector who knows the ways of gold and its corrosive effect on human character.

As Dobbs, Huston signed Humphrey Bogart. John Garfield was announced for Curtain, but Tim Holt took over his part. Huston cast his father for the key role of Old Howard, but asked the proud actor to discard his false teeth for the film.

"You should have heard Walter yell," says Evelyn Keyes. "It

took four people to hold him down while those dentures were being removed! After he saw some rushes of himself without the teeth he became reconciled—but he actually sulked for weeks over having to give them up."

Huston directed an early bar-fight sequence on the Warners lot, then prepared to take off for the wilds of Mexico.

On April 6 (the day Walter was 63) a DC-4 carrying the Hustons, Bogart, Holt and a crew of two dozen hand-picked technicians, left California.

The adventure began in earnest when fog lay so thick over the Mexico City airport that the pilot could not land. After five blind passes at the field he aimed for Vera Cruz, making an emergency landing there with near-empty fuel tanks.

"We finally got to Mexico City," says Huston, "where I was to hire my extras, since the script called for our gold hunters to face bandits and have a run-in with some villagers."

The Mexican in charge of the transaction told Huston that he could hire men on a daily rate for ten pesos per man, on foot, and fifteen pesos per man, on horseback.

"How much if they take a fall?" asked Huston.

"Twenty-five pesos, senor."

"I'll double that."

"Ah," said the Mexican, his face lighting, "for fifty pesos, senor, you can *shoot* them—in the arm or leg. But no killing!"

In Tampico, where Huston set up his camera for some street action, Bogart temporarily took over as the film's director in a sequence involving a character known as White Suit. John himself played this bit part of a rich American tourist.

"I really gave Johnny the works," Bogart was quoted. "Made him do his scene over and over and over. Got him mad as hell!"

Croves, Traven's hired "translator," was with them as they set out toward San Jose de Purua, 130 miles west of Mexico City, for the trek into the mountains. From the beginning, this little man took an active interest in every phase of the production.

It was here in Mexico that John Huston first became obsessed with pre-Columbian art. (The fact that he now owns one of the world's finest collections dates back to this trip.) In a cave near their shooting site an ancient Indian hiding place was uncovered, and

Huston dug out several priceless items which he eventually shipped back to the States.

John and Evelyn also took a 13-year-old orphan back with them. The active youngster, named Pablo Albarran, could not speak a word of English and had joined the unit as a water boy.

"Up to the time we got him," says Huston, "he'd been clawing to stay alive. When we took Pablo home it was great watching that kid grow backwards—from a young old man to a little boy."

The leader of the marauding bandits who attempts to steal the hunters' hard-won treasure was called Gold Hat—and for this colorful role Huston was using Alfonso Bedoya, a nervous Mexican who was obviously approaching a state of panic.

Huston knew that a substitution, at this point, was impossible— and be began talking to Bedoya in a soothing voice, his eyes looking directly, deeply into the Mexican's.

"After a while he had Bedoya believing he could successfully handle the role," says a crew member. "John had learned hypnosis in the Army and once, at a Hollywood party, he actually had William Goetz, the head of 20th, flapping his arms and crowing like a rooster."

Bogart was naturally the prime target for several practical jokes devised by Huston. The script required Bogie to stick his hand into a hole between some rocks. Huston had warned him to be careful of a Gila monster which had been darting about the terrain, and when Bogart felt tight jaws close over one of his fingers he let out an oath, yelling: "The damn thing's got me, John!" Of course the lizard was innocent; Huston had gripped Bogie's finger with a camera clamp.

Back at Warner Brothers, as outdoor location costs mounted on *Treasure*, Blanke had a difficult time calming studio brass. One particular sequence in which Bogart searches desperately for water had been four days in production. An unhappy Jack Warner sat through all four days' rushes in the projection room, then turned to Blanke: "If that son of a bitch doesn't find water soon I'll go broke!"

The studio had decided they didn't want Bogart to die at the end of the picture, but Huston and Blanke clung to their version— in which Dobbs is savagely murdered on the banks of a water hole by Gold Hat and his bandits. Blanke barely managed to keep the original ending intact after much wrangling.

In this scene Huston wanted a subtle mood of terror and menace to prevail, and kept rehearsing his cast endlessly, trying for "the right moment." The director told the Mexicans to stay close to the ground and to move when Bogart moved, to keep him ringed in. When one of the men executed a quick, ominous, centipede-like sliding movement down the bank toward Bogie—making the audience aware that death was inevitable—Huston nodded. "That slide was it," he says. "I knew then they had the feel of the scene, and we wrapped it up on the next take."

Under his son's direction, Walter Huston was turning in a flawless performance, and his only complaint was that "John ran me up too darn many mountainsides!"

During the months on location in Mexico Huston had been carefully observing the behavior of H. Croves. The furtive little man refused to have his photo taken, and made no comment when Huston told him that Traven was not answering any letters. As the crew headed back for California, having left Croves in Mexico City, Huston showed Bogart a rare photo he had finally uncovered of Traven.

"Do you recognize this guy?" he asked Bogie.

"Sure. That's old Croves. I'd know him anywhere."

There was now no longer any doubt in Huston's mind. The elusive author, wishing to maintain his vaunted privacy, yet unable to stay away from the filming of his novel, had assumed a false identity. The Croves-Traven mystery was solved.

Prior to the final scenes at the studio in Burbank Huston took his crew to Kernville, California, for a week and a half of "matching" shots. Even Kernville proved dangerous. Hairdresser Betty Delmont was almost trapped during a mine shaft cave-in at this site, but Huston pulled her free in time.

At Warners a Mexican mountainside had been recreated with 60 tons of earth and a miniature forest of transplanted trees. It was here that Huston would finish his picture, with a bandit raid on the mining camp.

Alfonso Bedoya, imported from Mexico, was now relaxed and confident in the role of the crazed bandit chief—and was, therefore, fodder for a John Huston Practical Joke. In his close-up studio shots Bedoya rode a plaster horse with an electronically-simulated gallop, and just prior to an afternoon's lunch break Huston told the actor he wanted "a final take before we eat." Alfonso wearily climbed back into the saddle, awaiting orders—but John suddenly called lunch and walked off the set. The Mexican was astonished, but when he attempted to dismount and follow Huston he could not. The plaster horse kept rocking up and down, up and down, with Bedoya firmly anchored in place. Huston had smeared triple-power glue on the seat of the actor's trousers.

The Treasure of the Sierra Madre was released in January of 1948, and was an instant hit. Time magazine declared it to be "one of the best things Hollywood has done since movies learned to talk . . . a magnificent and unconventional piece of screen entertainment . . . by turns exceedingly funny and completely terrifying." Critic Peter Ericsson stated: "The film is made with such intelligence and uncompromising savagery that one is astonished it was made at all . . . indeed it seems as though no other director could have tackled it."

Bosley Crowther, of the New York Times, summed up many reviews when he wrote: "Mr. Huston has shaped a searching drama out of the collision of civilization's vicious greeds with the instinct for self-preservation in an environment where all the barriers are down."

But it was James Agee who spoke most eloquently of the film. "This is one of the most visually alive and beautiful movies I have ever seen; there is a wonderful flow of fresh air, light, vigor . . . a fine athlete's litheness and absolute control and flexibility in every succession and series of shots . . . Walter Huston's incredible performance crowns a lifetime . . . John Huston's first movie since the war has been a long time coming, but it was certainly worth waiting for."

The tragic, ironic ending in Huston's moral fable—during which all the gold blows away on the wind as Old Howard laughs maniacally—was yet another variation on his stated philosophy: "The rewards of life are gained in the process of seeking a goal, not in the actual attainment."

Prizes and awards poured in. Huston won the New York Film

Critics Award for the best direction of 1948; and was voted best director of 1947–48 by *Film Daily*.

Treasure earned nominations in four Academy Award categories: for Best Supporting Actor (Walter Huston), Best Screenplay, Best Direction and Best Picture. Laurence Olivier's *Hamlet* won the Oscar as Best Picture, but John Huston beat out Olivier for Best Director, carried off a second Oscar for Best Screenplay—and Walter won the film's third Academy Award for his acting.

In accepting the Oscars, John Huston held up one of the gold statuettes and said: "If this were hollow and had a drink in it I'd toast Henry Blanke!" And the elder Huston, standing proudly beside his son on the platform, put a hand on John's shoulder. "A long time ago I brought up a boy," he said. "When he became a writer I told him one thing—'Some day you write a good part for your old man.' Well, by golly, he *did!*"

Chapter 6

TO TAKE A STAND

With the formation of the House Committee on Un-American Activities many Hollywood personalities became involved in the stormy Washington hearings. During 1947, when the probe was at its most active in the film capitol, writers and actors were summoned to Washington for testimony. Accusations and name-calling became the order of the day. The film world was getting a black eye—and John Huston, among others, felt that something had to be done about the situation.

In September of that year he met with William Wyler, Alexander Knox and writer Philip Dunne at Lucey's Restaurant in Hollywood to form the Committee for the First Amendment.

"We simply had to counter-attack this obscenity," he was quoted as saying after the meeting. "A man can't just stand still when rocks are being thrown at him."

By the third week in October Huston's group had added hundreds to its membership list. Accompanied by the Bogarts, Wyler, Paul Henreid, Danny Kaye and other luminaries, Huston boarded a chartered plane for Washington to present an official protest in force.

"It didn't do much good," Huston says, "but it gave us a secure feeling to be in there fighting for what we believed was justice."

The business of film-making continued—and Huston's next project was *Key Largo,* an adaptation of Maxwell Anderson's verse play. Richard Brooks served as collaborator in turning the rather ponderous, outdated stage vehicle into a workable shooting script. Jerry Wald produced for Warners with a strong cast: Bogart, Lauren Bacall, Edward G. Robinson, Lionel Barrymore and Claire Trevor.

Since most of the action took place within the confines of a Florida resort hotel on the Keys during a violent storm, Huston filmed all of his indoor scenes at Warners—although he did obtain some moody Florida location shots for the picture's early sequences. Robinson, in the role of a brash, brutal gangland lord, takes over the hotel with his hoods, holding the other characters at bay for 18 hours as the storm rages outside. Bogart's part called for him to "avoid trouble." He is finally driven into aggression at the climax, when he tackles the gang in a shoot-out on Robinson's boat.

Huston and Brooks, through the medium of Anderson's play, were making a comment on post-war America, attempting to prove in dramatic terms that a man cannot dispel his problems by avoiding them, that a stand must always be taken if personal freedom is to be maintained.

Key Largo took Huston 78 days to complete. He worked carefully to build a mood of heat, suspense and just-beneath-the-surface violence. His camera moved with each character the way the bandits had moved with Bogart—hemming them in, heightening the tension.

As a fading torch singer, in a role verging close to caricature, Claire Trevor had been beautifully instructed by Huston. "You're the kind of drunken dame," he told her, "whose elbows are always a little too big. Your voice is a little too loud, you're a little too polite. You're very sad, very resigned. . . ." He assumed a slouching stance at the bar, elbows thrust out. ". . . like this. Got it?"

Claire had it—and in fact won an Academy Award for her performance in *Key Largo.*

The *Nation* commented: "Huston and Brooks have almost completely rewritten Maxwell Anderson's play, and in almost every way they have sharply improved on it."

Despite the fact that Huston was now an unqualified success in Hollywood he was still considered a financial risk due to his attitude on money. "It just doesn't exist," he'd say. "You get this colored paper and you give it to someone and he gives it to someone else and that someone else gives it to someone else—so where is the money? It's just smoke in your hands. Nobody can get a grip on it."

Billy Pearson, a professional jockey and longtime Huston intimate, elaborated on this eccentric aspect of his friend's character. "At the studio John used to have his salary given to him each week in cash. I remember one week he was broke, as usual, and they handed him an envelope with five grand inside. 'You riding today, kid?' he asked me. 'Yeah,' I told him. I was aboard a real loser that afternoon and when I went by John's box I gave a kind of shrug, to let him know I didn't have a prayer. Well, he got it wrong—figured I was giving him an inside tip—and he laid every cent of that five grand on the nose of my 60-to-1 filly. After the race, as I was coming back past the stands, I saw smoke curling up. And there was Johnny, sadly feeding packages of tickets into the bonfire he'd started. That fire cost him five thousand bucks."

By 1948, after he had completed *Key Largo,* Huston was anxious to launch another project. He needed a personal loan of $50,000 to "clear the decks." When Jack Warner refused him the money Huston was stunned. Hadn't he been with Warners for 10 years? Hadn't he worked on a dozen films at the studio? Hadn't they invested almost three million in *Treasure?* Jack granted these facts, but would not consider the loan. That was that. No argument.

At a subsequent Beverly Hills cocktail party Huston encountered Sam Spiegel, a man he'd first met in the thirties when they had both been on the dole in London. Huston complained that the studio wouldn't advance "a measly 50 grand" on an extra picture commitment.

"You really want the money, John?"

"Hell, yes. *Sure* I do. But so what?"

"So I'll get it for you," said Spiegel.

"You do and I'll be your pal for life," Huston told him.

"How about being my partner instead? If I get you the money will you go in with *me* on that picture commitment?"

Huston agreed. If Warners didn't appreciate him he'd pull out. They shook hands on the deal—and the next morning Spiegel walked into the Bank of America and promoted the $50,000. He turned it over to John, then flew to New York and promoted $900,000 more on the strength of the director's name from the Bankers Trust Company.

This was the start of Horizon Pictures.

Spiegel, an innocent-faced individual with sad eyes, whose checkered career embraced cotton brokerage, a Mexican stage review and the draining of a swamp in Palestine, had been born in Austria and had first come to America in 1927. He returned to Europe in the early thirties, but was forced out of Berlin (where he was on assignment for Universal) when Hitler became a power in Germany. Shortly after this he met Huston in England. Now, upon forming this independent company, he changed his business name to S. P. Eagle.

Horizon's first picture dealt with a pre-World War II revolution in Cuba, and was originally called *Rough Sketch* (after the title of the book by Robert Sylvester in which this story was a segment). When Columbia studios entered the venture, as distributor, the title was changed to *We Were Strangers*.

John Garfield starred as Tony Fenner, a revolutionist who works with Jennifer Jones and Gilbert Roland in digging a tunnel into a cemetery where an attempt is planned to assassinate a high-ranking member of the Cuban government. Pedro Armendariz was playing the Cuban police official who threatens the operation.

Huston and his chief of photography, Russell Metty, were forced to match shots taken on Cuban streets with studio interiors, and it is to their credit that this was very cleverly accomplished. In place of *Key Largo's* Florida hotel much of *Strangers'* action centered in the tunnel, where Huston managed to create a potent claustrophobic effect with his fluid camera.

In adapting the Sylvester story Huston collaborated with Peter Viertel (the writer who would later publish a controversial novel in which a thinly-disguised Huston would figure as the savage lead character). Their screenplay, in the tradition of earlier Huston efforts, highlighted a struggle for personal liberty combined with an ironic climax in which the whole exhausting endeavor fails to come off. (The Cuban official cancels his visit to the cemetery.) A fierce gun battle winds up the film, and Garfield dies cradling a smoking machine gun, to the words of Calypso-singing Roland: "Tony Fenner died for me—and now I have my liberty."

Although tightly directed, with excellent performances from Roland and Armendariz, the picture was flawed. As a British critic pointed out: "Huston introduces a cogent moral paradox: can violence be justified by a non-violent purpose, or is existentialist action the end in itself? But this paradox is never resolved, and the final result is inconclusive."

Time labeled it "murky . . . but above average." *Collier's* praised it as "a picture Columbia may well be proud of." But the *Hollywood Reporter* bitterly attacked it as communist-inspired. "A shameful handbook of Marxian dialectics," they fumed. ". . . and the heaviest dish of Red theory ever served to an audience outside the Soviet."

Huston was openly amused by this wild allegation, and quoted the *Daily Worker's* angry charge, printed just a week later, condemning the film as "capitalistic propaganda." Huston told the press: "I'm proud and delighted to have both of these lunatic ends converging on me."

The *Nation* had another complaint about *We Were Strangers:* "Huston is a crazy man with death; he pockmarks a story with gratuitous deaths, fast deaths, noisy deaths, and in idle moments his characters play parlor games with gats . . . and he is forever calling on his characters to prove that they can soak up punishment, carry through harrowing tasks, withstand the ugliest taunts . . . Everything must be done the hard way."

In the same month that *We Were Strangers* was released (May, 1949) Huston received the One World Award for his contributions as a film director to world unity. He immediately announced plans to make a round-the-world documentary in which he would roam the globe, "seeking the corporate image of humanity." United Nations agencies would act as his sponsor. No doubt he was sincere in this plan, but the trip was never made. ("Instead, I signed a contract

with M-G-M and got bogged down in *Quo Vadis*. As for world unity
—well, I couldn't even maintain the unity of my own family.")

Huston's third marriage had collapsed—and Evelyn Keyes was
no longer living with him at the 480-acre ranch in San Fernando
Valley.

Announcing their separation, Miss Keyes cited animals as one
of her main problems in living with Huston. "I'm allergic to fur—
and he's got a regular *zoo* out there," she told reporters. "Each day I
had to share my husband with monkeys, horses, dogs, cats, parakeets,
goats, pigs and a burro named Socrates. When he brought home a
chimp, that was the beginning of the end. The chimp wrecked my
boudoir, smashed three valuable Mexican vases and tore our lace
curtains to shreds. And none of the monkeys were housebroken,
which sure didn't help."

John merely remarked: "I taught that girl to play a sweet game
of billiards."

What really concerned Huston was the result of a personal bet
he'd made with Evelyn in an effort to bypass California's community-
property law. With a divorce in the wind, Huston knew that his
favorite set of hand-carved Incan figures would have to be divided
between the couple. "Baby, I'll flip you double or nothing for 'em,"
he offered. Evelyn accepted the bet, and won, taking the whole set.

Billy Pearson tells a similar story, but with a different ending:
"John owned a rogue filly named Bargain Lass. He was desperate to
get a win out of her, but she was rough to ride and would try and
flip over on her jockey at the starting gate. I told John that I'd
guarantee to win on her—providing he'd give me my choice of anyone of his pre-Columbian figures, including the group he'd found
himself in that cave up in Mexico. He didn't like my terms, but
agreed that I could have my choice if I won on Bargain Lass.

"Five days later I entered John's filly in a race, wrapping her tail
over the back bar of the starting gate to keep her from flipping. I
knew she had the speed if I could just get her clear. I did—and won
easily.

"John heard about it at the studio and rushed home to beat me
there. We both arrived at the same time. I saw him run inside the
house, grab several figures, and dart into his bedroom with them. I
was right behind him, yelling, 'No, you don't, Johnny. I want my

pick of those!' He gave me a defeated look and said okay, to go ahead. So I picked one. 'You sure that's the one you want?' he asked. 'I'm sure,' I told him. Then he let out a big howl of triumph and led me back into the living room. Turns out he'd grabbed all the second-rate figures, knowing I'd *think* he was taking the best. So I ended up with the poorest of the lot!"

Huston's deal with M-G-M provided that for $3,000 a week he would direct and help write a spectacular new screen version of *Quo Vadis*, with his father in the role of St. Peter, starring Gregory Peck and Elizabeth Taylor. The film was due for a Rome start in early July of 1949. But in May, because of an eye infection suffered by Peck, the studio cancelled its plans for the Italian trip. (The rainy season in Italy would delay shooting for several more months.)

This was actually a fortunate turn of events for Huston—since he and producer Arthur Hornblow, Jr. decided to embark on another film while waiting for *Quo Vadis* to get underway. They chose a bitterly-realistic novel by W. R. Burnett (the author of *High Sierra*) about big city crime entitled *The Asphalt Jungle*.

Huston's screenplay, prepared with Ben Maddow, treated this subject as "a left-handed form of human endeavor," and probed deeply into the lives of those men and women who ply their dark trade in the iron jungles of the city. Discussing the basic concept of this film, critic Eugene Archer wrote: "Huston has increasingly focused his attention on a handful of characters in conflict with their environment—small people in a big world . . . Here he penetrates the masks of a group of criminals engaged in a million dollar jewel robbery . . . to reveal an assortment of human vices; alcohol, greed, lechery, self-pity, all examined with a dispassionate objectivity which accepts the human condition without apology or embarrassment . . . The laws these men follow are determined by jungle ethics, with the potential rewards of wealth and luxury qualified by the interminable threat of death . . . Huston's doomed protagonists cannot expect salvation and cannot hope to avoid the fate which has become the core of their existence . . . The long robbery sequence . . . introduces a chain of accidents which precipitate the disintegration of the group, a result clearly foreshadowed by the earlier scenes."

As a master criminal (who plans the caper) Huston chose his old friend, Sam Jaffe; for the feminine lead, an unknown stage

actress named Jean Hagen; for the gang's crooked lawyer, Louis
Calhern—and for Dix Handley, the hood who is hounded by drink
and bad luck, Huston wanted Sterling Hayden. M-G-M didn't. Hayden was not box office; he was fighting his own alcoholic problem,
was under the care of an analyst. The big studios didn't trust him.

Hayden tells the story of his tryout for the role: "When you're
greeted by John Huston, you know what it's like to be met. You
step into his office, and it is full of people and smoke. The moment
Huston sees you he swings to his feet, his eyes on you alone. You
suddenly sense that simply by coming here today you have relieved
this rangy man of some immense burden. You are the one person he
wanted to see at 2 P.M. sharp. . . . He clears the room, then says: 'I've
admired you for a long time, Sterling. They just don't know what to
make of a guy like you in this business. . . . Now, I want you to do
this part. The studio wants a top name star, but this is my picture
. . . and I want you in it.' . . . After I did the scene, giving it everything I had, John made just one remark: 'If anybody ever says you
can't act—have 'em call up Huston.' I knew I was in."

One more role remained to be filled: the lawyer's mistress—a
girl who could combine sex-appeal with a kind of vital innocence,
who could be soft yet instinctively cunning. This was Angela.

Lucille Ryman, onetime head of Metro's talent department,
came to Huston with the name of a young blonde who would be
"just perfect for Angela." The girl was Marilyn Monroe. A bit
player, she had no speaking roles to her credit—and when she appeared for her interview in Hornblow's office she was extremely
nervous; her hands were shaking as Huston gave her the script.

"Listen, kid, don't worry about this," he told her. "Just take it
home and look it over, then come back when you're ready to give
me a reading."

Marilyn was back in three days with the part memorized. She
had two scenes in the film. In the first of these, Angela is seen
stretched out on a divan. But there was no divan—or even a couch—
in Huston's office.

"I'd like—to—read the first scene on the floor," she said, blink-
ing at Huston. He looked amused.

"Sure, dear, anyway it feels right to you."

Kicking off her shoes, Marilyn eased to the carpet, reclining there while she acted out the scene. Then, before Huston could comment, she asked if she could try the scene again. He nodded. After the second runthrough she stood up, nervously awaiting his reaction.

Huston smiled broadly. "You didn't *have* to do it twice, honey. You had the part on the first reading."

With *The Asphalt Jungle* Huston took a major step forward as a creative director-writer. This picture won him two more Academy Oscar nominations and a 1950 Screen Directors Guild Award. As one British critic wrote: "The structure of this film is more complex than anything Huston has previously attempted, and it is expressed with an advanced technique commensurate with his material—it is the work of a director at his technical peak and at the height of his intellectual involvement with contemporary society."

What was becoming known as "a Huston ending" climaxed *Jungle*: the robbery attempt failed and Dix, the broken criminal, seeks his own green Kentucky meadows in which to die.

"I credit Greg Peck for this one," said Huston. "We'd have been stuck in Rome, doing *Quo Vadis*, if Greg's eye infection hadn't come along."

For Marilyn Monroe, it was the beginning of international fame —and a road that led her, more than a decade later, to star in *The Misfits*, her last completed film.

In December of '49 Hornblow and Huston finally stepped away from *Quo Vadis*, leaving it to other hands.

"Arthur and I just couldn't spend any more time on this," the director declared. "We both had other pictures waiting for us."

In Huston's case, the new project he tackled became one of the most controversial efforts of his career: for M-G-M he was to direct Stephen Crane's Civil War classic, *The Red Badge of Courage*.

Chapter 7

AN UGLY WAR AT M-G-M

White-haired, viper-tongued Louis B. Mayer, head of Metro-Goldwyn-Mayer studios in 1950, hated all that was ugly and loved all that was beautiful. He loved Andy Hardy and loud technicolor musicals and any story featuring a kind-hearted mother. He hated most European films because they were dark and damp and full of ugliness and nobody sang or danced in them. And they all too often contained what he termed (with contempt) "stark realism."

To Mayer, the work of John Huston represented stark realism. "That *Asphalt Pavement* thing," he would say, "is full of nasty, ugly people doing nasty, ugly things. I wouldn't walk across the room to see a thing like that."

Dore Schary, then the studio's vice-president in charge of production, served as Huston's buffer. Schary had activated *Quo Vadis*, going over Mayer's head to New York and taking up the matter with

Nicholas Schenck, president of Loew's, Inc., who was the financial power behind the throne at Metro.

Mayer had always wanted a loud, colorful, DeMille-like *Quo Vadis* brimming with strong men and innocent maidens, but Schary had insisted on a modern treatment, in which Nero would be presented as a symbolic Hitler killing off Jewish martyrs. This was the film Hornblow and Huston had been prepared to make. Upon their withdrawal, Mayer happily turned the vehicle over to Sam Zimbalist and director Mervyn LeRoy, to get *his* concept of *Quo Vadis* onto film.

With *The Red Badge of Courage* Schary was again backing a project to which Mayer was firmly opposed. "That old classic book full of blood and killing has got no laughs, no songs, no entertainment value," he told Schary. "Who else but a man like Huston would want to make a thing like that book?"

Actually, it was Gottfried Reinhardt, a producer with M-G-M since 1940, who had first suggested Crane's story to Huston. They had taken the idea to Schary, and he had presented a screen treatment to Loew's New York office, where it was approved by Schenck. Mayer gave in; he would go along with them if they were set on doing the picture, but he had no faith in *Red Badge*. ("It will be ugly and not make money.")

Schary was excited about the idea of transferring Stephen Crane to the screen. "This can be an inspiring picture," he said. "It can bring honor and prestige to M-G-M. And John promised me it wouldn't cost too much. A million five tops. Which is not too much."

Huston also promised to complete the picture in 43 days: nine days of rehearsal, 34 days of filming. Star costs would be eliminated since the director wanted "fresh faces." The Youth he had selected, Audie Murphy, was the little infantry hero who had turned to acting after the war. Cartoonist Bill Mauldin would portray the Loud Soldier. Character actors would fill out the other main roles in the cast.

"Courage is the real star of our picture," said Reinhardt. "The boy is wounded, and wears a 'red badge of courage' in battle after he conquers his fear."

The plotline of Crane's book was simple: The Youth, sickened by death, runs from battle—then regains his courage and leads his comrades in a charge against the enemy. He becomes a hero, and his soul is cleansed in this bloody baptism of fire.

"Fear in a man is something tragic or reprehensible," Huston said. "But fear in a youth can be ludicrous. We'll show this. Our film should have real humor in it along with the horror of battle. And I want to put in some things I've learned about war."

When Mayer heard that there would be no stars in *Badge,* nor any women, he threw up his hands. "I would rather shoot Huston than shoot this picture. We could then put the money into a defense in court. No jury would convict me."

Reinhardt and Huston had planned on taking their cast and crew to Nashville for location work, but finally settled on doing the entire film in California. They would spend two weeks in Chico, near the Sacramento River north of San Francisco, then complete the action (mainly the battle sequences) on Huston's ranch 30 miles from Hollywood.

As Huston explained it: "A particular location isn't important to this film. Our battleground will be abstract, representing no actual Civil War site. The Youth really has nothing to do with the outcome of the Civil War—he simply gets tossed on the roulette wheel of battle, gets thrown off and, of his own free will, jumps back on again. This could happen to a boy in any war, anywhere, and that's what we'll show. That's what the picture will be about."

After a salary increase Huston was now being paid $4,000 a week by M-G-M, and had been guaranteed $28,000 more for adapting Crane into screenplay form. But he was so deeply in debt ("The ponies keep me broke!") that he required an advance of $150,000 from the studio, which they reluctantly agreed to give him.

In February of 1950, he used part of this money to obtain a quick divorce in Mexico. Huston had fallen in love with Enrica "Ricki" Soma, a beautiful ballet dancer and former New York model.

"I'd originally met Ricki during the war when she was still a child," says Huston. "She grew up, got her photo on the cover of *Life,* and came to Hollywood. Then Jennifer Jones re-introduced us at a Selznick party. I don't think her father much liked the idea of our getting together."

Mr. Soma, who ran Tony's Restaurant in New York, expressed his candid view of Huston to writer Alfred Bester: "This man has no respect for money or for women," said Mr. Soma. "With me, love and money are sacred. They should never be abused. John Huston is reckless. He is accustomed to going his own way. He has no consideration for others."

Ricki was openly enchanted with her director, and accompanied him everywhere. "John's very sweet and gentle," she said. "He's like a child."

Huston had been in the midst of preparing *The Red Badge of Courage,* when he decided to divorce Evelyn Keyes and marry Ricki. He began the screen treatment on the plane to Mexico, obtained his divorce on February 10th at Juarez, married Ricki on the following day at La Paz, then finished dictating the treatment on the flight back to Hollywood.

Walter Huston's death, that April, left John stunned and shaken.

"The best friend he ever had was his father," said James Agee. "And that feeling was thoroughly reciprocated. It was a rare, fine thing to see a father and son so irrepressibly pleased with each other's company and skill."

The nine days of rehearsal for *Red Badge,* conducted at Huston's ranch, went smoothly. John had planned on directing the film from horseback until he found that "it was too hard on the horse." To save shooting time a special "leapfrog" system had been devised, wherein a substitute director would set up one shot for Huston while he was off directing another. (This was to prove impractical, since Huston never knew exactly how he wanted a shot arranged until he got to it.)

The 92-page screenplay on *Red Badge* took Huston five weeks to write. Two thirds of the dialogue came directly out of Crane's book: Huston was determined to remain faithful to the novel.

Because one of the major scenes specified a river crossing, involving some 250 Union soldiers, Huston and Reinhardt had chosen the Chico location to begin shooting their film. The immense park in Chico would serve admirably as the forest setting, and the Sacramento River could be used for the crossing.

Looking over the men who had volunteered as extras in Chico, the director was not satisfied. "We need tougher guys," Huston told an assistant. "Go out to the pool halls and service stations and bars and get me tough guys. Young, tough faces—and plenty of 'em."

Then Huston went fishing with Audie Murphy.

Eight of the tough guys collapsed from the heat during the first day of shooting in Chico's 2400-acre park—and Reinhardt reported that the insurance people were worried about some of the Chico boys drowning in the river. Reinhardt said he would personally cross the river, alone, to make certain it was safe. Huston said fine; producers were expendable.

To get one minute of screen drama, 250 of Chico's toughest guys crossed the Sacramento River under Huston's direction. Nobody drowned.

Reinhardt was very pleased with the early rushes. "Even Margaret likes them!" he told Huston. Margaret Booth was M-G-M's executive film cutter, and her word carried weight in high places.

Huston was working carefully with Audie Murphy as the focal point of the film. He had seen in the 26-year-old veteran a mixture of sensitivity and latent strength needed for the Youth. "He's a gentle-eyed little killer," Huston said of Murphy. "Why, in the war, he literally went out of his way to find Germans to kill. Gottfried and Dore didn't want him at first, but I changed their minds. God, Audie won every metal there was: the DSC, Medal of Honor, Silver Star, Legion of Merit, Bronze Star, Purple Heart, Croix de Guerre . . . you name it, he won it. This gentle little guy. Wow. Greatness is often a matter of quality rather than ability. Dad had it. So has Audie. You take a great horse. Go past his stall and you can feel the vibration in there. Audie is like that. He vibrates."

Two of the most important scenes in *Red Badge* were the deaths of the Tattered Man (Royal Dano) and the Tall Soldier (John Dierkes). It is in the Youth's agonized reaction to these deaths that Crane's view of war becomes eloquently clear. Huston spared no effort to make them memorable—and both actors contributed superbly to the final effect.

The forest footage completed to his satisfaction, John and the crew headed back for his valley ranch that September to begin filming the battle sequences.

Huston was striving for what he called "the Brady touch"— scenes in the manner of the great Civil War photographer, Matthew

Brady, a man the director very much admired. "I've got a Brady of my great grandfather," Huston proudly told Reinhardt. "He was an officer in the Union Army—Colonel William P. Richardson. My mother kept his sword. I'm letting the Youth's general wear it."

The violent Confederate charge, from which the Youth would flee, was budgeted at $16,469—and the Youth's initial look at war, at his first battle, would cost M-G-M $155,000—none of which impressed Huston.

"Hell, they're putting eight and a half million into *Vadis*," he said. "One of the ballet numbers in Art Freed's new musical is costing them 400 grand. And in our battles we're using more extras than *Gone With the Wind!* They're getting off cheap."

Huston, in Army suntans, a red-and-green checked cap slanted over one eye, directed the fighting with zest and untiring enthusiasm, yelling out his commands as 200 Union troops, Murphy at their head, charged down a long hill into a sea of smoke and cannon fire. Stunt men pitched from their horses; wagons were overturned; musket shots filled the California air. Reinhardt said it all looked great.

"Just like a Brady, eh, kid?" yelled Huston.

One of the extras, a wrinkled M-G-M veteran, said that he had been in all the cinema wars and that this was the roughest. "I been in the Napoleonic Wars and the Spanish-American War and the Second World War. I was a foot soldier in the American Revolution. Fought the Philistines in *Samson and Delilah*. Fought the First World War in *Sergeant York*. Was in the Irish Rebellion in *Elizabeth and Essex*. Even fought the Civil War once before—in *Gone With the Wind*. But this one is the roughest!"

As Huston's War progressed, film costs mounted. Already they were nearly $50,000 above the budget, but John dismissed such problems. He was nearing the finish of what he felt was the best film he had ever made. Each segment must be perfect, with no detail overlooked.

For a bit part in the production, in which he would taunt Murphy as a ragged fellow-soldier, Huston pulled on a dusty blue uniform and smeared mud over his unshaven face. Reinhardt told him he looked wonderful, and the scene was shot, with a final close-up of Huston's jeering face.

"The only son of a bitch who is uglier than I am," Huston said as he watched the rushes, "is ole John Dierkes. He's so ugly he's beautiful. I just love to use ugly faces."

Margaret Booth told Reinhardt she would work with him in rough-cutting *Red Badge* while Huston was busy finishing the film on location. During the first showing of the pieced-together footage she criticized a digging scene over which Huston had taken great pains. "I don't like it. Cut it. Cut it to the bone," she said. Miss Booth found other faults and suggested further cuts. "The marching scenes are too long," she said. "A lot of stuff can go."

Reinhardt said he appreciated her help.

Huston was nearly finished with *Red Badge* when Reinhardt went out to watch him shoot the fierce Confederate bayonet charge from which the Youth flees.

"It's gonna look like the real thing, Gottfried," said Huston.

Reinhardt said that Mayer would hate it because it would be filled with stark realism.

"Well, it's an ugly war, Gottfried. That's what the book is all about. Death isn't pretty."

"It is at M-G-M," said Reinhardt. "In *Quo Vadis* it will be lovely. Even the lions will have pearly-white teeth."

Huston grunted, and prepared to start his scene.

All the gray-clad extras were ready to charge. Murphy was ready to flee. The smoke machines were turned on, and the explosives were set for detonation. The ground was littered with corpse-dummies. Huston finally yelled "Action!"

With a chorus of rebel yells, the extras charged down on Murphy and his comrades, bayonets thrust forward through the smoke, while Huston and Reinhardt watched behind the camera. "I would run from this!" said Reinhardt, as Audie bolted.

Sam Spiegel was on location that afternoon and he told Reinhardt: "I get Johnny next! On *The African Queen*. We're doing it for Horizon. It'll make a lot of money. All in color. We're after Bogart."

Reinhardt grunted.

The Red Badge of Courage ran four days beyond the promised schedule, but Dore Schary seemed delighted that Huston had come this close to the original estimate.

"We'll maybe end up a hundred grand over budget," said Huston. "But we have some *wonderful* stuff, Dore."

The cast had gifted Huston with a hand-tooled leather saddle in gratitude for his work on the film, and Murphy told a reporter: "Anything I do good in this picture is because of John Huston. I'm not an actor—but John gets what he wants out of me. He guided me all the way."

Aided by Benny Lewis, Reinhardt worked over the second rough cut of *Badge,* then showed some 40 minutes of footage to members of Loew's advertising staff. "We must sell this as a *great* picture," he said to them. "Another *Good Earth* kind of thing."

Later, Reinhardt told Huston he was concerned about making a profit from *Badge.* "It's so damned *artistic,* John!"

Huston didn't seem worried. Tryst, one of his stable of thoroughbreds, had been running out of the money, and *this* annoyed him. He'd bought a new filly from Calumet Farms and hoped it would run faster. "God," he said, "someday I'll have a good winner— and then I'll be able to say 'Well, you bastards, this is what it was all about!' Luck and the right kind of breeding—that's all I need."

Huston went duck hunting with one of the film's stunt men after winding up *Red Badge,* and when he returned he sat down with Reinhardt to look at the edited footage, running 78 minutes. He liked what he saw, but Reinhardt was disturbed. "John, it has a major flaw. No story. There is no real story in this picture."

Huston agreed that it needed some additional work, perhaps a new scene or two in camp with the Youth. They'd lick the story problem. He made no comment about the fact that his own bit part had been cut away, along with other footage.

Dore Schary also told them it needed "more story."

On the next showing ten minutes had been added—but the Youth was still not clear enough as a person to suit Reinhardt or Margaret Booth.

It was now November, and Huston had been on *Red Badge* for over nine months. Spiegel was hounding him to begin writing *African Queen.* Ricki was a mother, and had presented John with a son, Walter Anthony Huston. James Agee would soon be flying in from New York to collaborate on the new script. Preparations had to be made for a trip to the Congo where the film would be shot.

"I've gotta leave Metro," Huston told Reinhardt. "Too much is piling up. I'm going over to California Studios, to Horizon's office, and work there. I can't cut *Badge* with you. But keep me informed."

James Agee, the writer Huston chose as collaborator for *African Queen*, had already demonstrated solid ability with an impressive script on Stephen Crane's short story, *The Blue Hotel*. John had been considering this project as a possible follow-up to Crane's Civil War novel, but the idea was dropped. The two men had become friends during the many weeks it took Agee to write a profile on Huston for *Life*—and both were equally enthused about bringing C. S. Forester's novel to the screen with Bogart and Katherine Hepburn as their two leads.

Agee's introspective approach occasionally irritated Huston and once, during the period when they were outlining the film, Agee was trying to prove that the trip taken by the man and woman down the Congo river symbolized the act of love.

"Hell, Jim, tell me something I can understand in concrete terms," snapped Huston. "People on the screen are gods. They are symbolic of life, but they are not life itself. You can't have symbolism within symbolism. You must *show* what they do and feel, not hint at it."

For directing *Queen*, Huston was guaranteed only $2,500 a week—as against M-G-M's $4,000—but he would share in the profits through his percentage tie-in with Horizon.

To Reinhardt, Huston's lack of concern over *Red Badge* was disheartening, since he now had serious doubts about the commercial possibilities of their film. By January of '51, when Huston and Agee were well into the new script, working together at a ranch in Santa Barbara, Reinhardt called from M-G-M to sing the score of *Red Badge* over the phone.

"Isn't it great, John? Bronislau Kaper did it. Shows what goes on *inside* the Youth. We're really getting to know that boy!"

Huston agreed that it was indeed great—then put down the phone and went back to work on the script of *Queen*.

At 41, Jim Agee was not a strong man, but he drove himself at a killing pace on whatever project involved him. Trying to keep up with the inexhaustible Huston, he suffered his first heart attack that year (an ailment which would cause his death in 1955). Each morning before breakfast at the ranch, John played three vigorous sets of tennis ("to tune up the system"). Agee, who had not played for some time and was not in condition for it, made a strenuous effort to match Huston shot for shot. During one of these early-morning workouts he collapsed on the court.

Warned to "take it easy" by the doctor who tended him, Agee was incapable of following such advice—and he stayed with Huston on the script in an effort to have it completed by the time John left for Africa.

In February, having received the fully-scored print of *Red Badge*, Reinhardt set up a special advance screening for Huston, William Wyler, agent Paul Kohner and the cast. After it was over Wyler congratulated John for a "wonderful job." Reinhardt was beaming. "The death of the Tattered Man is terrific," said Wyler. "Just terrific." Everyone else thought so too. They all told Huston what a great picture he had.

Two nights later, hours before the film was due for a Sneak Preview at a theater near M-G-M, Huston and Reinhardt ran off the print for Dore Schary at his home. Schary told them they had a great picture. "It's gonna stand up for years!" he said.

That evening *The Red Badge of Courage* had its first showing before a general audience. Louis B. Mayer was sitting in the theater; he had not as yet seen the film. People laughed at the death of the Tattered Man. When Murphy bolted at the Confederate charge several patrons bolted from the theater. During one of the more violent battle sequences Mayer abruptly turned to a stranger next to him and snorted: "That's Huston for you!"

By the film's end, 32 people had walked out. Some of the preview cards read "Lousy" and "This stinks." And although a portion of the audience had responded well to *Badge,* a mood of heavy gloom prevailed in the lobby. Margaret Booth said coldly: "They *hated* it." Louis B. Mayer did not say a word to Huston or Reinhardt; he walked directly out to his waiting car and was driven quickly away.

"At least Hedda Hopper liked it," Reinhardt remarked sadly.

On the following evening a second preview was held in Pasadena, with Huston and Reinhardt attending. The audience consisted mainly of teenagers who jeered and hooted Murphy as he ran from the advancing bayonets. The death of the Tattered Man elicited howls.

"God!" said Huston after the shooting. "I'm glad I'm going to Africa tomorrow!"

Reinhardt said that narration would certainly have to be added, informing the people that this was a classic film from a classic book.

"I think it's my best picture," Huston said. "How could they hate it so much?"

"These kids never *heard* of the Civil War. So they want jets and we give 'em muskets," Reinhardt sighed. "They *laugh* at cannon balls."

With Huston on the way to the Congo, Reinhardt and Booth and Schary all went to work cutting and re-arranging *Badge*, and dubbing in a narration from the book (spoken by actor James Whitmore). After another public preview, in which the response was somewhat better, Schary decided to cut out the death of the Tattered Man. "No one will miss it, doll," he said to Reinhardt. "The Tall Man dies; that's enough."

Sequences were shifted so that the two main battles became one. Murphy was seen wearing a bandage on his head at the start of the fighting, was seen without it in the middle, then had it on again at the end. But no one seemed to notice or to care about this at the fourth preview.

A defeated Reinhardt wrote to Huston in Africa, telling him that many of the key scenes that built the picture up to the feeling Crane had in the novel were now gone forever. He said that he had tried to keep it intact, but had failed.

The cost of the film had reached $1,640,000.

Louis B. Mayer, angry with the New York office and feeling that they were unjustly favoring Schary, resigned from Metro, leaving the studio in late August. He had been firmly opposed to releasing *Red Badge* in any form—but within a month after Mayer's withdrawal Schary brought the film out in New York.

Huston's faith in the job he had done was substantiated by the critical ecstasy which his film engendered. Even in its final, cut-down form (69 minutes) much of the quality and power Huston had put into the film remained.

"Adhering to Crane's characters and his theme, John Huston has discovered for all time how to make a printed page come alive on the screen," wrote Arthur Knight in the *Saturday Review*. "Bids fair to become one of the classic American motion pictures," said *Newsweek*. The New York *Times* called it "a major achievement"—and the *Tribune* found it "chokingly filled with powder smoke and animal terror."

"*The Red Badge of Courage* has been brought to the screen by the brilliant John Huston as an offbeat motion picture," observed the New York *Morning Telegraph*. "This is a strangely exciting work, unique in the recent history of the movies."

The New York *Mirror* said that it was "a memorable war saga and a wonderful example of modern film art."

In England, when the film arrived overseas, a British critic rated it as "an impressionistic, sometimes surrealistic view of war as seen through the eyes of an innocent young soldier . . . containing one of the finest battle sequences ever filmed, and many eloquent cinematic details."

Only a few sources carped about the redundant narration being "ill-advised and intrusive."

The *Film Daily* placed it on a list of the five best-directed pictures of the year—and the National Board of Review named *Red Badge* the second best picture of 1951 (behind George Stevens' *A Place In the Sun*.)

Yet Reinhardt had been correct in his concern over its commercial possibilities; due to poor opening business in New York, *Red Badge* was relegated to the lower half of a double bill featuring Esther Williams in one of her gaudy underwater epics.

"*Badge* never made much money," admits Huston, "but my *next* one sure did."

Huston's next one was *The African Queen*.

Chapter 8

GOD! SAVE THE QUEEN!

For Humphrey DeForest Bogart, the adventure began with a phone call from John Huston: "Hey, old son, I have a great property. The hero's a low-life, and since you're the biggest low-life in town the part is therefore ideal for you!"

Bogart asked for details.

"Kid, we've got Katie Hepburn and we're making the whole damn thing in the Congo. Darkest Africa! It's really going to be something, you and me down there with the king pythons and the bull elephants. You're going to love it!"

Bogie later told a friend: "Before I met the Monster my range was Beverly Hills to Palm Springs. Maybe 120 miles. Now Huston wants me to fly 12,000 miles into the Congo. And the crazy part is, I've agreed to go!"

Mrs. Bogart (Lauren Bacall) was coming along "for the ride," and Huston said he'd meet them all in Stanleyville.

Huston was flying to England for business discussions—and to get properly outfitted for the trip.

"God, those English bootmakers!" he says. "They put *love* into their boots. They lavish great care and affection on every pair. Whenever I'm in London I head straight for Maxwell's to order some."

Another Huston "must" in London is F. Tautz, of New Bond Street, whom the director refers to as "the best sporting tailor in the world." When Huston first appeared in the shop and told George Dingle, chief of the firm, what he wanted in the line of suits, the man was shocked. Huston had sketched a jacket with long, flaring tails to be nipped in smartly at the waist, and drainpipe pants which were tightly molded to hug the legs; the whole affair was to be set off by a red-and-green Tattersall-checked vest with lapels and brass buttons.

"But, sir, this is neither lounge suit nor hunting suit," protested Dingle. "It is neither."

"It is what I want," said Huston. And it was what he got.

Now, in February of 1951, Huston went to Tautz' for some shooting jackets and twill riding breeches, then to Maxwell's for a pair of soft maroon jodhpur boots.

He next phoned Peter Viertel in Switzerland, for some help in polishing the final script on *Queen*. "Just stuff at the end mainly," he told Viertel. Could Pete come to England? Fine, fine.

At a business meeting with Sam Spiegel and Horizon's London backers Huston was warned about the extra costs and problems of shooting *Queen* in color. But Huston stood firm on its use in order to give the film an extra element of richness and appeal; color would guarantee half a million more at the box office. It was worth the trouble.

Roads were discussed. Moving supplies and heavy camera equipment into the Belgian Congo was a massive undertaking as most roads were little more than narrow, rutted paths between encroaching walls of jungle. Huston told them he'd scout all locations by air and pick out the proper sites. He wanted to find a dark, winding body of water to correspond to the one described in the book.

(The geography of the novel was faulty, in that Forester had his boat traveling downriver into what was presumed to be Lake Victoria. Factually, African rivers do not run into the great lakes but away from them into the sea. Huston would, however, stick with the author's plotline, reversing nature.)

As Forester told it, the story took place during the First World War, and concerned a tough, ragged bush veteran, who ran a small mail boat in the Congo, and his highly improbable adventures with the prim and proper daughter of a missionary.

Films and Filming outlined the action: "After her father is killed, Rose and Charlie are trapped by the Germans in British West Africa, but rather than surrender, they determine to take action against the enemy with the only means at their disposal, the mail-boat (called the African Queen) and a supply of raw explosives which can be used to destroy the German gunboat which guards the mouth of the lake near Kenya. The action involves a voyage down an uncharted, all but unnavigable river over rapids and marshes, past a German fortress in the dilapidated old boat, which is rapidly falling to pieces, under constant menace from nature and a hostile enemy, with no other assistance than their own initiative.

"This seemingly impossible, supremely arduous journey resembles the heroic efforts of other Huston protagonists: the miners' trek in *Treasure of the Sierra Madre,* the revolutionaries' tunnel in *We Were Strangers,* the jewel thieves' attempt in *The Asphalt Jungle* and the soldier's painful return to his regiment in *The Red Badge of Courage.* . . . That they are eventually successful in their mission is a testament to human endurance and a triumph over the worst that man and nature can provide."

Says Huston: "For a while there, Agee and I thought we might let them fail, but we got to like these two characters so much we changed our minds. We decided to let 'em blow up the gunboat."

In order to find his river, Huston logged 25,000 flying miles over dense jungles, endlessly crossing and re-crossing the Dark Continent. At last he found just what he had been seeking: the Ruiki, a Congo river which was ink-black as a result of decaying vegetation. Aside from snakes and poisonous insects, the Ruiki was infested with parasitic worms, known as Bilharzia. They caused a lingering disease which was, according to Huston, "worse than anything the crocs could do to you." This is doubtful, since the active, always-hungry crocodiles could do quite a lot, but the Bilharzia were certainly to be avoided.

The Ruiki, then, was ideal.

Huston cabled the Bogarts and Hepburn to let them know he'd found their location site, then set about buying several elephant rifles and books on big-game hunting.

"Boy!" he said to Viertel. "This is really going to be something, isn't it? Ever shot an elephant, Pete?"

Viertel said that he hadn't, and didn't want to; he'd finish polishing the script at Entebbe, then head back for Paris or Switzerland, where there were no elephants.

"Okay, kid," Huston sighed. "Me, I'm going after a big tusker. Hell, they've got everything in the Congo . . . buffalo, antelope, leopards, lions, hippos—even guinea fowl." He told Viertel that only death would stop a charging buffalo.

Huston was now wholly caught up in the lore of the Congo— 5,000 square miles of impenetrable jungle stretching beyond the tip of Lake Albert, an area nearly as large as the United States, harboring death in every form, from giant pythons to flesh-eating plants. Hemingway country.

"After we shoot our footage on the Ruiki," said Huston, "we'll move up toward the headwaters of the Nile."

Viertel wondered how Miss Hepburn (described by the Hollywood press as "dainty") would like Africa. Huston didn't know, but thought he could handle her.

As his cast headed for Stanleyville, Huston went on safari—and wrote his wife (who was then living in Malibu Beach with their son) to tell her that he had not as yet bagged an elephant, but had stood right next to a herd of them and that this gave him "a very funny feeling." He also informed her that a lion had feasted on some local natives not so long ago, but that he had not personally run across any lions as yet.

From the moment Katherine Hepburn arrived in Africa she found the country "utterly divine." She looked forward to seeing a bamboo forest, and was impressed by the masses of brilliantly-colored flowers outside her living quarters. It was all "so terribly charming."

Katie was not so charmed to learn that the leprosy rate among the natives was nearly 70% and that the syphilis rate was 100%—or that 10-foot pythons were not uncommon in the jungle. Or that

African ant hills were often 50 feet high. Huston decided to save the news about the worms until later.

"I *had* to do this film on location," Huston stated. "I wanted these characters to sweat when the script called for it. On a sound stage you fake it, but in Africa you don't have to *imagine* that it's hot, that it's so humid and wet that cigarettes turn green with mold; it really is hot and clothes *do* mildew overnight—and when people sweat it isn't with the help of a make-up man. Africa was the only place to get what I was after."

Bogart swore he would drink only Scotch during the trip and that he would avoid all African dishes. "Scotch and canned beans—that's my recipe for survival." Lauren Bacall was unhappy about the fact that she could not obtain an African tan due to the killing intensity of the sun. "You'd just obtain African third-degree burns, honey," John told her.

When Miss Hepburn found out about Huston's attempts to bring down an elephant she coldly accused him of being a potential murderer. What's more, she objected to alcohol—and had heard that Huston drank as much or more than Bogart.

"That's true, dear," he admitted. "But you must take the bad with the good. On the Ruiki, we're all going to be in the same boat."

Actually, there were two boats: the small, steam-powered Queen, looking exactly as Forester had described her in his novel, and a large raft, designed to hold thousands of pounds of equipment and lights as well as Huston's 34-man technical crew from Britain. The raft was actually three boats in one, formed by strips of planking laid over native pirogues.

With his full company aboard Huston supervised the official launching—but when the craft reached mid-river it began to sink.

"Bail out the pirogues!" John shouted. "Then get this thing back to shore and dump all the hitch-hikers!"

In their enthusiasm the Congo natives had overcrowded the raft, and weight was a problem.

"There were *many* problems," Huston says. "For example, Katie had always been used to her own dressing room back in Hollywood and expected the same privacy on location. So we rigged up a kind of portable palm leaf affair, but it didn't last long. I think the pole collapsed. She finally just got dressed out in the bush."

For the film's early sequences, a camp had been built on the banks of the Ruiki, complete with bucket-showers and a bamboo dining room. Lauren Bacall was the company cook, declaring herself an expert at python soup (which Bogart did not think was funny).

From their first scenes together, Hepburn and Bogart added a special comic dimension to the picture which surprised Huston. "I didn't expect it," he admitted. "One brought out a vein of humor in the other, and this comic sense, which had been missing from the book and screenplay, grew out of our day-to-day shooting. Of course, humor underlies the story, and was behind the action, but it was the offbeat combination of Bogart and Hepburn which enabled this element to emerge."

With Jack Cardiff manning the color camera, Huston was getting some excellent jungle footage. And the Congo natives were not the only curious observers on hand to watch the crew at work; thousands of chattering monkeys peered from trees along the river.

"We had this one older group of baboons," says Huston, "who'd come down to the shore and squat there each afternoon, just to watch us shoot. They were a great audience—better than most critics I know—and after a scene we'd look over at them to check their reaction. Sometimes they'd clap for us. I tell you, kid, we all got so we dreaded the day those baboons would shake their heads!"

With several sequences remaining to be filmed, torrential rains fell, forcing the troupe indoors. Waiting out the downpour, Bogart and Huston gleefully attacked the supply of Scotch. They winked at Hepburn, roared out a lusty drinking song, then exchanged lewd Irish jokes in a calculated effort to shock the actress.

"You boys believe you're being awfully wicked, don't you?" she snorted. "Well—you don't know what the word 'wicked' means!"

The two men looked confused. "Now, what the hell is she driving at with *that* crack?" Bogie asked.

Huston shrugged. "I dunno—but I *think* she's one of us!"

The social ice was broken; Katie was in.

"She turned out to be a wonderful sport," stated Huston. "Just loved Africa. And despite her misgivings about hunting, she became my staunchest safari companion. Katie didn't use a rifle, but she knew how to aim a camera—and she'd stand fast when elephants were stampeding and advance, with only a 16-mm camera in her hands, on a forest pig which stood four feet at the withers and could lay a man wide open with one thrust of his foot-long tusks."

Back at work after the rains had ended, Huston faced a major disaster: the Queen had sprung a leak, and was rapidly sinking. Shouts of "God! Save the Queen!" failed to alter the situation—and the mailboat settled heavily to the bottom of the river.

It took the crew (assisted by 150 natives) three days to bring the Queen back to the surface. The heavy boiler which powered the boat was raised via makeshift pulleys attached to overhanging trees— and a mechanic was summoned from Ponthierville to get the sensitive steam engine running again.

A frightening situation developed which led Huston to change his plans about remaining for any length of time in this part of the Congo. Late one night the camp was awakened by howling, torch-bearing natives.

"We were in our hut," says Lauren Bacall, "and Bogie started to get out of bed. He put his foot on the ground and felt something moving; he slapped at his pajamas—and I could see that the floor of our hut was alive with ants. Since the legs of our bed stood in cans of kerosene, we were safe for the moment, but it was a ghastly feeling."

An army of safari ants was on the march, eating their way across country, and only fire could stop them. These insects were flesh-eaters, and could quickly strip an animal—or a man—to the bone. Driven back by the torches, they stubbornly returned the next day, forcing Huston to abandon the campsite.

"It's their jungle," he said. "If the owners want to take possession the tenants will just have to move."

Huston loaded the Queen on a flatcar, then boarded the ancient woodburning train for Stanleyville. A plane took them to Entebbe, in British Uganda, where the troupe played cricket, losing to a local team 51 to 160. (Unaccountably, Bogart was the star of the game.)

"I got all I needed on the Ruiki," said Huston. "We'll head for Lake Victoria, then along the Nile. The big tuskers are up that way."

Worried about delays in the production, Spiegel cabled Huston that he was flying in for a conference.

"I thought we were leaving," said Bogart.

"We are," Huston told him. "I know how to get rid of Sam. Leave him to me."

When Spiegel arrived at the airport Huston greeted him warmly —and so did 100 chanting, drum-beating natives. They cried out: "Wel-kum Sam! Wel-kum Sam!" Endlessly. Spiegel couldn't get away from them. They followed him everywhere; the chanting and drum-beating were continuous. "It's no use, Sam!" Huston said. "You're too popular here. We can't talk business now. Go on back to London and I'll meet you there soon."

Spiegel took the next plane out. Huston paid off the natives he'd hired to torment the producer—and calmly prepared to resume his picture.

Not all African natives trusted Huston. Near Lake Albert, when he attempted to hire workers, the Africans fled in horror. John later found out they had been warned that white men from Hollywood were cannibals.

"Our home for the next five weeks was an old sidewheel paddle steamer," says Lauren Bacall. "It was woefully inadequate, but at least the ants couldn't get to us."

Awaiting supplies and equipment which were due in by truck, Huston explored the lake country. Among its attractions was a dense mahogany forest—and Huston was invited to witness the felling of one of the giant trees. The ceremony promised excitement, and the Bogarts agreed to accompany him into the forest. For an hour, they watched native laborers sawing away at a massive trunk as the sky darkened.

"Looks like rain," said Huston.

This was an understatement. The sky seemed to rip apart; a torrent of water was loosed, and veined lightning danced overhead.

"Let's get *outa* here!" yelled Bogart.

"We can't leave yet," shouted Huston. "Not until our tree falls!"

Lightning forked down, sizzling through the sudden darkness. With an immense bone-cracking sound, one of the mammoth mahogany monsters swayed, then swung earthward in a great arc, thundering to the forest floor a few feet from Huston and the Bogarts.

"That wasn't even the one they were sawing!" Bogie shouted. "The whole lousy forest is coming down on our heads!"

They sprinted for the car, reaching it as fresh bolts of lightning stabbed into the trees.

"Boy, I'm sure sorry Katie had to miss *this*," said Huston as they gunned away.

The actress was battling illness—and assistant director Guy Hamilton was also stricken. Suffering a nervous collapse, he was flown back to London. Several other crew members had contracted dysentery.

Anxious to resume shooting, Huston arranged for native drummers to beat out reveille each morning at 6 A.M. Action now centered on the burning of a native village. The thatched huts were ignited at Huston's order, causing great consternation among the natives, who were certain that the whites were crazy. Who but crazy people would build a fine village only to burn it down?

The troupe now moved up the Nile, toward Murchison Falls, for more location shots—but Hepburn's illness caused the director to call a four-day shutdown. If Katie had not improved by then, Huston would head back for London.

The Bogarts went hippo-hunting with their cameras, and Huston tried to bag his elephant, without success. A hill of empty Scotch bottles testified to his frustration.

Hepburn recovered—but the final location scenes were filmed under trying conditions; nine members of the British crew had to be sent home. Dysentery and malaria were decimating the Queen's ranks. Only Huston and Bogart remained in excellent health throughout the ten weeks in Africa.

"The bugs don't bite me," Huston said. "I bite them."

Back in London, where he would spend two more months finishing *The African Queen*, Huston ordered a jar of leeches brought to the set. Bogie was visibly shaken. "You're not gonna really put those damn things on me, are you, John?"

"Absolutely," said Huston. "I want you to shudder as you burn each of them off with the tip of your cigarette. Now, kid, you just *wouldn't* shudder if the leeches were phony."

Bogart shuddered—and this scene was among the most memorable in the film.

Released through United Artists, *The African Queen* became one of 1952's top moneymakers. Critical reaction was typified by the remarks of Eugene Archer: "The hilarious adventure of a dissipated tugboat captain and a strong-willed missionary's daughter, deriving its comedy from the rich and complex interplay of two of the screen's great comic characterizations, emerges as one of the most original films ever made . . . Like Chaplin's masterful comedies, it is deeply moving, and funniest when it is closest to tears . . . Humphrey Bogart's portrait of the gallant, helpless Charlie, who gradually acquires pride in his own capacities, is a magnificent *tour de force* which admirably complements Miss Hepburn's performance while achieving a unique comic dignity of its own."

For his role in *Queen*, Bogart won an Academy Oscar—and Huston was nominated for Best Director and as co-author of the Best Screenplay.

"It's like I said, kid," John jubilantly told Bogart, after the awards. "Real leeches pay off in the long run!"

Chapter 9

HUSTON'S PARIS

During his stay in Africa Huston had read *Moulin Rouge* by Pierre La Mure, a novelized biography dealing with the life and times of the famed French artist, Henri de Toulouse-Lautrec. The book excited Huston, since he had been looking for a proper way to dramatize Lautrec's tortured life; this novel provided the frame he needed.

Huston's first choice for the role of the crippled, dwarfish painter was Jose Ferrer, and John phoned the actor in New York to ask if he had read La Mure's book.

"Have I read it? I *own* it," Ferrer told him. "I plan to do it for the stage, and I've got the author working on a play version right now."

"Forget the stage," snapped Huston. "This thing has got to be done for the screen—in color, on the streets of Paris, with interiors at Maxim's and the Deux Magots. I'll get Tony Veiller to do the script. We'll fill it with can-can girls in black stockings and music and brothels and champagne! With you as a bearded dwarf in a top hat. Well, kid, what do you say?"

Ferrer said yes—and Huston made immediate preparations. He moved his family into a rented chateau at Chantilly, near Paris, and contracted Oswald Morris to work out a new method of color photography.

"I want to get the essence of Lautrec on film," he told Morris, "I want it to seem his paintings have come to life in front of the camera. Can we do it?"

Morris thought it could be done. With Vertes, the fashion artist, and Eliot Elisofon, a noted color-still photographer, Morris worked out a method whereby standard colors could be muted through the use of special filters.

While the preparations for *Moulin Rouge* were underway Huston grew restless. John wired his jockey pal, Billy Pearson, inviting him to the chateau. He told Billy that he had imported an Irish thoroughbred, and that they could train the horse on the steeplechase course at Chantilly. Then Pearson could ride him under Huston's colors.

No American jockey had ridden in France for over two decades, and Pearson was the object of intense curiosity when he arrived in Paris. Huston threw a party for the leading French riders at Le Signe Royal, introducing Pearson as a "fierce contender."

"By 3 A.M. we were all happily drunk," recalls Huston. "So it seemed a good idea to go out and jump some fences. Luckily, no necks were broken."

Since Billy would be competing at Longchamp, Huston took rooms at the Lancaster Hotel in Paris. Each afternoon he would go out to the track with a taxiload of fellow-Americans to watch Pearson ride.

Unfortunately, the local jocks had decided to teach Billy that Frenchmen win French races—and each time the American rode he was bumped and elbowed and blocked. He could never get near the lead horses.

Pearson's loyal supporters, led by Huston, were rapidly losing their money. A sizable number of U.S. dollars vanished with each race, and Huston vowed to change all this.

"Listen," he told the group (which included Art Buchwald, John Steinbeck, Gene Kelly, Anatole Litvak and a lovely Paris model named Bettina). "I've got an idea. Let's give these boys some of their own medicine. Now, Billy rides in the Grand Prix de Saint James next week, and no matter what has to be done to accomplish it, he is going to win!"

The group plotted Pearson's epic ride in detail. He would issue Rebel yells, use his boots and elbows, and foul every jockey he could reach. When the race was over, if the crowd attacked Billy, Huston would set fire to the main grandstand in order to create a diversion—affording Pearson a chance to escape.

The plan worked beautifully. Billy became a tiger; he used every trick in the profession to gain ground, flinging his mount against other horses to throw them off stride, shouting insults, blocking on turns. Leading the pack, he crossed the wire to win as the angry French crowd roared its displeasure.

"Naturally, Billy was disqualified," says Huston, "Every jock in the race protested him. He was booed off the track. It was wonderful. And we didn't even have to burn down the grandstand."

That night Pearson was feted by the Americans for his sterling performance, and champagne toasts were raised to his courage and endurance.

"The next day Johnny promoted 100,000 francs from a rich Greek," says Pearson. "He used the money to have a statue done in bronze— of me winning the Grand Prix de Saint James."

Huston enjoyed prowling the city's art galleries with Pearson in search of items for his private collection. There was one particular Monet painting in a Left Bank gallery which Huston had purchased for $10,000 earlier that season. Now, after his series of losses at Longchamp, Huston was broke—but Pearson told him not to worry. "I'll get us some eating money," he promised. "Let's head for the gallery on the Left Bank. I want to talk to the guy who runs it."

Confused, Huston agreed. He waited outside while Billy conversed with the owner. A few minutes later the jockey emerged, waving a check for 300,000 francs. "I told him I was your agent, and demanded 10% as my commission on his sale to you. Told him you were stinking rich and would buy more paintings from him only if he cooperated. So I got the dough. Now let's eat."

The filming of *Moulin Rouge* began in late June, with Huston producing as well as directing. "I am trying to learn all the things Sam Spiegel was born knowing," he wrote a friend, "and I find it pretty tough going."

To duplicate the physical stature of Lautrec, Huston devised a "torture rig" for Ferrer, which could not be worn for more than half an hour without cutting off the circulation in the actor's legs. Ferrer would slip his knees into a pair of scuttle-shaped boots filled with cotton wool which supported short, artificial legs, reducing him from his normal 5' 10" to Lautrec's stunted 4' 8"—and when Jose faced the camera the effect was quite startling.

"I could even walk this way," says Ferrer, "but after an hour or so with this rig on I'd have to have my legs massaged to get the blood flowing again."

Co-starring with Ferrer in the film were two French actresses: Colette Marchand, as a young prostitute with whom Lautrec is involved, and Suzanne Flon, his lost love. Zsa Zsa Gabor was set to portray Jane Avril, the exotic cafe entertainer who inspired Lautrec's most famous poster.

The fashionable, bejeweled Zsa Zsa had been selected by James Woolf, a British producer who was associated with Huston on the project, and John was not happy with the choice. When Miss Gabor appeared on the set to meet Huston he scowled at her. "Come upstairs," he snapped. She followed the director into a large, deserted dining room.

"Sit down over there," he said, "against the wall."

Huston walked to an open window and stood beside it in the din of afternoon traffic. Horns blared; motorcycles coughed and roared; trucks clashed their gears. "Okay," he said. "Let's see what kind of a voice you've got. Read your lines."

Nervously, Zsa Zsa began to speak.

"Louder. Project. I can't hear you."

She tried again. Huston looked dour. "Again," he commanded.

"I was shouting at the top of my lungs," she recalls. "Sweat was soaking my dress. It was nightmarish, and it seemed to go on forever."

Huston finally dismissed the blonde actress, but told her to report back the next day.

"I knew we'd have trouble working together," says Zsa Zsa, "but at least I would be in one of the most glamorous pictures of the year. It would be worth the trouble."

Since a great many outdoor scenes were to be shot at night, Huston had to make arrangements for this with city authorities. A reporter from *Figaro*, one of the largest papers in France, got wind of Huston's plan—and ran a headline story which was completely false.

"The paper said we would happily pay 20,000 francs to anybody whose sleep we disturbed," relates Huston. "By the next morning, we had hundreds of letters from people in various neighborhoods, begging us to shoot our night stuff along their streets. Naturally, we got *Figaro* to run a retraction."

One citizen of Paris was so outraged over the fact that she would not be receiving 20,000 francs that she declared war on Huston. Each time the director began a scene she'd bang a big metal pot against the wall. The racket was ear-shattering.

"We located an old fortune teller," says Huston, "and bribed her to go tell the woman that if she didn't stop banging pots against walls she'd end up cursed with bad luck. The French are very superstitious, and this did the trick. We never heard a peep out of her after that."

David Mage, assisting Huston in setting up the complex street scenes, marveled at the director's ability to blot out the modern world.

"Here we were in front of the Deux Magots on a busy Saturday in the middle of a blistering Paris summer, in 1952, trying to create a scene out of the 1800s," Mage related. "On the right of the square was a five-way intersection, and on the left a three-way intersection. The whole area—45,000 square feet—had to be cleared of all cars, bicycles, motorbikes, buses, pedestrians and animals. For this we had a task force of 30 policemen and three assistants, plus three men in charge of the extras who doubled as auxiliary police. We had 150 extras, a trio of horse-drawn carriages and a horse-drawn van running around in the square. Traffic was backed up for three miles in all directions. And there sat Mr. Huston, perfectly composed, with a kind of soft little smile on his face; for him this was Paris in the Gay

Nineties. He'd personally erased every trace of the modern world—and you could tell he was pleased by the feat."

Huston was far less pleased with Zsa Zsa Gabor. Her accent annoyed him almost as much as her lack of projection.

"Goddamit, you're dropping the ends of your sentences again," he would tell her. "Zsa Zsa, if you go dead once more at the end of a line I'll personally murder you, so help me!"

"Like dog and cat we fought each other," she says. "I tried to explain to him that the Hungarian language is spoken with a sing-song lilt. I am Hungarian, and Hungarians are inclined to drop the last word of every sentence. But he would not try to understand. He just sipped his vodka and said, 'Again. Do it again!' My big scene, where I sang the theme song of the film, he made me do over at least 50 times!"

Huston was equally determined regarding costuming. On one occasion, in the midst of a late-night session, he shut down the set for almost two hours in order to obtain a feather boa. Huston had his crew running through the side streets of Paris searching for this item while his production manager sobbed with frustration. The boa was eventually purchased from a female impersonator in a Pigalle nightclub, and Huston calmly resumed shooting.

Generally, the director was pleased with Colette Marchand, but during a tricky sequence at the Pre Catelan restaurant, when the actress was instructed to quarrel violently with Lautrec, Miss Marchand's performance failed to satisfy Huston. He wanted her to register nervous anger—and deliberately began goading her. She flounced off the set, but instead of going after her Huston kept everything in readiness. He waited.

David Mage reported the outcome: "When she returned, Colette was still extremely nervous and angry at Huston—but these feelings were repressed, and she was smoldering under an internal pressure. On this take, since her personal feelings corresponded to the scene, she performed wonderfully."

On Bastille Day, July 14, Huston gave his entire cast a holiday. He invited them all to dine with him at his favorite restaurant, Tour d'Argent, overlooking Notre Dame. Zsa Zsa was enchanted with this gesture, particularly in view of the fact that she was introduced to Aly Khan that evening. The Huston-Gabor battle had ended.

"John really became a darling man," she says. "When I finished my part in the film he drove me to the airport in his special hunting clothes. He knew I was wild about horses, and the sweet thing had gone to all the trouble of putting on this wonderful riding outfit from Tautz, just to see me off. It was very touching."

Milton Berle was among the numerous visitors to Huston's Paris that summer. The comedian was engrossed in one of Ferrer's scenes when two husky gendarmes suddenly grabbed him. "Is this the one you told us about?" they asked Huston, who nodded in seeming relief. "Glad you got him. He's extremely dangerous."

As Berle was being handcuffed, he quietly pleaded: "I know it's a great gag, John. But tell 'em to take it easy on me, willya? I've got a weak back."

"You should have thought of that before turning to a life of crime," said Huston. "I'm afraid it's far too late for pity."

Berle sighed in defeat as they carried him away.

"We had one visitor we never saw," says Huston. "That was Pablo Picasso. It wasn't until we'd finished shooting that I learned Picasso had been near the set every day for the three weeks we were on location. Someone tipped him off as to where we'd be shooting each afternoon and he'd rent a room in a house or hotel there and peek out and watch what was going on. Maybe he thought seeing what the movies were doing with Lautrec would be some kind of clue to his own future fate. It was tantalizing as hell to find out he'd been spying on us all that time."

The superb color photography of *Moulin Rouge* proved to be the best thing about the film. Technicolor had initially objected to Huston's revolutionary use of their process, writing strong letters in an effort to persuade him to stick with proven methods. "At first they just couldn't see what we were trying to do," he says. "We wanted the color hazy in some places, sharp in others. According to mood. We were after a tonal range which would correspond to oil paint. It drove 'em crazy, but later they wrote again, mightily impressed after they'd seen the results, to ask us how we did it. Part of the secret involved using big gelatin filters in front of the set lights to soften the overall scene."

It took Huston nine more weeks to complete *Moulin Rouge,* and while he worked on the final print he discussed the possibility of filming *Matador*, Barnaby Conrad's novel, with Ferrer in the starring role. This failed to materialize, although Huston still expresses his fascination with the art of bullfighting. (He once entered the ring on a dare, barely escaping the horns. "There was absolutely no art in the way I got out of that bull ring!")

Although Academy Award members thought enough of *Moulin Rouge* to nominate it as Best Picture (and Huston as Best Director), the reaction of the critics was anything but warm.

"A purely superficial treatment of Lautrec's life and times," wrote Peter Barnes. "There is an appalling lack of depth . . . this is probably the worst-acted film to come from a major director in the last decade."

Hollis Alpert called it "a dimly-realized portrait . . . representing the artist chiefly as a haunted, forlorn, lonely man, carrying a torch for a dismal prostitute . . . the effect of the whole . . . is soporific. Ferrer can be blamed for a poor performance . . . but Toulouse-Lautrec was hardly the lugubrious oddity presented by Huston."

Films and Filming began by praising the color technique: "The photography is Huston's most significant technical achievement . . . in that it creates a tangible artist's world inhabited by stylized figures who might have emerged from an Impressionist's canvas. As a setting for the drama of Toulouse-Lautrec, Huston's structural design is magnificent . . . and in the unforgettable opening can-can sequence, the composition flows vibrantly into life. Unfortunately, while the form remains, the substance soon vanishes. In concentrating on visual images, Huston neglects their motivational purpose, and in a facile and superficially-acted script the figures remain sketches on a canvas. The battle of form and content is finally shadow-play."

But Huston was not around to absorb the critical blows. He was occupied with a new love.

He had discovered Ireland.

Chapter 10

IRELAND AND THE DEVIL

Among landed Irish gentry, fox hunting is a beloved sport. The sea-green hills beyond Dublin, broken only by occasional walls or fences, stretching in soft rolling waves to the horizon, offer ideal terrain for a brisk gallop behind baying hounds. Here ride the Black and Tans and the Killin' Kildares—and, by 1953, John Huston was riding with them.

He had brought his family to Ireland late the previous year, renting a huge Georgian country house near Kilcock, 30 miles from the River Liffey in County Kildare. This was Courtown, designed to serve as Huston's base of operations for future trips around the world. His daughter, Angelica, was born there in '53, and Ricki shared her husband's enthusiasm for Irish soil.

"God, but it's a wonderful place for a man to go when he's tired of fighting traffic and taxes," states Huston. "The country is simply beautiful, and the people are straightforward eccentrics. No nonsense about it. It's the only place where you can get drunk and not wake up the next morning with a guilty conscience. In fact, drunkenness in driving is a mitigating factor over there. They sort of shake their heads and say, 'Well, you know the poor fellow was under the influence. You can hardly hold him to blame for a bit of an accident.' It's delightful and fantastic."

One of the first things Huston did after unpacking his suitcases was to rush out and buy several hundred dollars' worth of fox hunting gear. He knew nothing whatever about the sport, but was determined to learn as quickly as possible. John's horsemanship saved his life, since jumping Irish hedges after a fox can be extremely dangerous for a novice. Despite his cavalry training, John was often pitched from the saddle. ("After awhile you get used to spills. Adds spice to a hunt.")

In Ireland Huston was content. There were horse shows, the Leopardstown races, good whiskey, hunting dogs, trout streams and witty companions. The life of a country gentleman ideally suited him, and for a long while none of the villagers realized that a great "fillum" celebrity had come to their green land. Additionally, Courtown provided Huston with the space to stable his thoroughbreds, in support of his belief that "a horse is the most beautiful animal God ever fashioned."

However, his prime business was picture-making, and he was seriously considering a film which would be shot near his new home in Ireland, to star Burl Ives as a wandering minstrel of the early eighteenth century. As with *Matador*, it did not come to fruition. Instead, Huston again joined forces with Humphrey Bogart on a modern adventure drama set in Italy.

Bogie owned the property, a book by James Helvick entitled *Beat the Devil*, which the actor felt could be another *Maltese Falcon*. It dealt with a gang of international criminals involved in a uranium swindle, and seemed to contain all the necessary elements of suspense, danger, and romance. Bogie phoned Huston in Paris about it.

"I'll get Tony Veiller started on a script," said Huston. "And Pete Viertel to work with him. Pete's good on this sort of thing."

Thus, *Beat the Devil* became a three-way collaboration. While Veiller worked in Venice, Huston polished in Ireland and Viertel final-drafted in Switzerland. After three months, when the script had been completed, Bogie called Huston to give him a reaction: "It stinks," he said. "I can't do it."

"Nonsense, we're due to start filming in Italy right away," said Huston. "Meet me in Rome and we'll talk about a rewrite."

Dispiritedly, Bogart flew to Rome. He had a copy of a Hollywood trade paper in his hand. "Read this," he told Huston. "Tells all about the new 3-D craze. We'll lose our shirts if we film this thing in flat black and white."

"But we've got Gina Lollobrigida," said Huston. "And Gina's not flat! She's got built-in 3-D."

"Be serious, John. We're in trouble all the way down the line with this turkey."

"First," said Huston, "you can forget 3-D. Just a fad. It'll pass. Second, I have contacted Truman Capote and he's coming here to work with us on the script. Third, I found a great spot to shoot the picture—Ravello, high above the Amalfi Coast south of Naples. An old pirates' lair. Only way to the top is by goat trail! I spotted it during the war. Marvelous view. Now, cheer up and let's get cracking."

Bogart was the unofficial producer, since he was personally investing $600,000 in the project, but all the final decisions were made by Huston. This included casting—and John's penchant for "fresh, ugly faces" resulted in his hiring an offbeat assortment of Italians, most of whom had never seen a motion picture camera. The only other "names" in Devil, beyond Lollobrigida and Bogart, were Jennifer Jones, Robert Morley and Peter Lorre. The latter two were to portray international crooks. Lorre, recently recovered from a long illness, had become fat and white-haired since his Falcon days. Morley was happy to have a starring role as the leader of the gang after his bit part as Hepburn's missionary father in African Queen. Miss Jones was on hand to provide Bogart's love interest. Bogie would essay his usual tough, cynical role as an American adventurer married to an Italian wife (Gina).

"Capote will meet us in Ravello," Huston told Bogie. "The two of us will go on by car to Naples. I want you to see some of this country, amigo. Takes your breath away."

Bogart reluctantly climbed into the car with Huston. He didn't quite trust the director, since upsetting things invariably happened to him whenever he was with John—but a quiet, scenic trip along the Italian coast promised to be relaxing.

"The only trouble was, we had this crazy Italian behind the wheel," relates Huston. "He even made *me* nervous."

The driver was a man who hated to make decisions. When he came to a fork in the road, he could not decide whether to go left or right. Thus, he went straight ahead—through a three-foot stone wall into a ditch. Bogie reeled out of the crash with two loose teeth and a split tongue; Huston was unharmed. "Drove us right smack through the wall," Huston said, shaking his head in amused disbelief. "The Italians are an amazing people, eh, kid?"

Bogart glared at him. His opinion of Italian drivers did not need to be verbalized.

As promised, Capote met them at Ravello. Accommodations for the cast and crew were divided between the Palumbo Hotel and an out-of-season villa. The area had just one telephone, and to reach the village itself, where most of the scenes would be filmed, required infinite patience. The road seemed to twist endlessly upward, as one ascended via muleback. Bogart, who did not like mules, nonetheless rode up on one each morning from the villa, a look of intense displeasure on his face.

The script which Bogie had disliked was thrown out, and Capote began with an entirely new approach. "What we had as our base was a straight adventure melodrama—which was impossible to take seriously," he said. "John and I decided to kid the story, to treat it as parody. Instead of another *Maltese Falcon,* we turned it into a wild satire on this type of film. Due to my late start, and the schedule John imposed, I was rarely more than two days ahead of shooting with my scenes."

As filmed, *Beat the Devil* was nearly incomprehensible, and playwright Harry Kurnitz described it perfectly when he wrote: "No matter where you come in during its running, you seem to have missed at least half the picture."

Morley, Bogart and Lorre were after uranium; Jennifer Jones was after Bogart; Gina was after Jennifer's husband; the police were after all of them. Also in on the proceedings: a mad, drunken ship's captain, a homicidal little man called The Galloping Major, a ruthless Arab chief who resembled Groucho Marx and a fat, pouting chauffeur whose antique car plunges into the sea.

"We sort of lost Helvick's novel along the way," admits Huston. "But we had a hell of a lot more fun making the new version."

Bogart was given such lines as: "I'm only in on this because the doctor told me I needed plenty of money. Without money I become dull, listless and have trouble with my complexion."

Jennifer's reaction at seeing Morley and his gang at the beginning of the film was also typical: "Those must be very desperate men, because they walked right past and didn't even look at my legs!"

Miss Lollobrigida (nicknamed Frigidaire by Bogart, who claimed he was "not a bosom man") was confused by much of what went on at Ravello. The American sense of humor was a mystery to her, Huston's in particular. She spoke her lines phonetically, with a heavy accent, and seemed dazed by the succession of rapid-fire scenes.

"Don't underestimate her," Huston warned Bogart. "She has nine lawsuits going right now in Italian courts. Gina's a solid addition to our picture, mainly because she reminds you of a modern apartment building—the kind with outside balconies."

The evenings at Ravello were given over to poker, with Huston and Bogart dominating the table. Their main victims were Capote, who lost 200,000 lira to them, and Robert Capa, the famous still photographer who was in Italy to take publicity shots for the film.

"Capa was the worst poker player in the world," says Huston. "Even worse than Capote. He didn't cost us anything. We won his salary back each night."

Another off-set pastime was judo. Capote, a very small man, claimed that he could immobilize Bogart merely by pinning back his arm. Bogie pretended to be helpless and in great pain whenever Capote surprised him from behind with this armhold, confiding in Huston that he could actually squash Capote "like a bug on a wall." After one of his scenes had been completed Bogart was talking to Morley when his arm was suddenly pulled up behind his back. He winked at Morley and began to groan loudly. The pressure increased, and Bogie let out a real howl, twisting his head around to face his antagonist. Capote was nowhere in sight; Huston had decided *he* would try the armhold.

While shooting *Beat the Devil* in Italy Huston aided the anti-communist cause by hiring his men exclusively from "free" unions. Many non-communist members of Red-dominated groups joined the "free" unions in order to work for Huston, thus helping to break the Red grip on Italian labor.

Billed as a "gangster-adventure" by United Artists, the film was not a moneymaker. Moviegoers expected another rough-and-tumble Bogart thriller, and got tongue-in-cheek satire instead. Bogie himself dubbed it "a mess," but most critics found the film delightful. The *Saturday Review* called it a brilliant parody, and *Time* found it to be "as elaborate a shaggy-dog story as has ever been told." Praised by the *New Yorker* as "hugely entertaining," the reviewer added that "Huston's new picture flashes with a kind of bright lunacy."

In England the reception was cooler. *Films and Filming* termed *Devil* "an act of self-indulgence," and berated Huston for allowing himself to make such an off-trail production. "It is a private joke, amusing only to the initiated . . . a film for connoisseurs, who will treasure it highly—most highly perhaps, because it is valueless for the layman . . . Divorcement from one's audience in a medium as commercially oriented as the cinema must be considered a dangerous trend."

As usual, the director had left his critics far afield. He was now in full pursuit of his greatest quarry, the elusive White Whale; he was after *Moby Dick*.

Chapter 11

THE GREAT WHITE WHALE

When Ray Bradbury's *The Martian Chronicles* was published by Doubleday, in 1950, the author sent John Huston an inscribed copy. Just out of his twenties, Bradbury was rapidly gaining a reputation for high-quality science fiction, and this book solidified his leading position in the field; it offered an imaginatve, bitter-poetic look at man's life on Mars some hundred years in the future. Huston liked the book, and expressed interest in bringing it to the screen. The two men exchanged letters over the next three years, and Bradbury continued to send Huston his latest stories as they were published.

"I'd seen and admired every John Huston film," says Bradbury, "and had told him that I felt we were destined to work together. Sure enough, in late August of 1953, when Huston was in Hollywood editing *Beat the Devil*, he phoned from his hotel asking me to drop by. I was naturally excited, thinking that perhaps he was ready to talk about doing the *Chronicles*."

At the hotel Huston studied Bradbury with deliberate care, as a potential buyer studies a new car. "You ever been overseas?" he asked.

"No," said Bradbury.

"Ever written a screenplay?"

Bradbury said he hadn't.

"Well, how would you like to come to Ireland and write *Moby Dick?*"

The author was stunned. "I—I don't know. I'd have to think about it."

"Take your time. Make a decision and let me hear from you in the morning."

Bradbury walked out to the nearest bookstore and bought a copy of Melville's classic.

"I'd never read the novel," he admits. "As a boy, I'd tried it and given up. Now, as a man, I wondered how Melville would affect me. I couldn't work on a book to which I didn't respond emotionally. Going to Europe as a script writer for Huston would be tremendous, but not unless I possessed the self-confidence needed for so huge a project."

In Melville, who worked a century behind him, Bradbury found a kindred spirit.

"By sheer luck, I opened the book at Melville's chapter on the great spout of the White Whale that fountained on the mysterious sea at night . . . then I came upon the chapter which details the ghost color of the whale . . . then to Ahab's monologue on its being a mild day with the wind smelling as if it blew from the shadow of the Andes . . . I read all night—in a fever of excitement—and called Huston the next morning to accept his offer."

Melville had been tried before; two other screen versions of *Moby Dick* had been released, both starring John Barrymore as the mad Captain Ahab. (In 1926, as a silent, it was called *The Sea Beast,* but when the book was dramatized again in 1930 Melville's title was restored.)

Huston had originally envisioned his father in the pivotal role, but now he had to find a substitute Ahab. The film would cost a great deal of money, and Warner Brothers had agreed to finance it providing a star name headed the cast. They were worried about the fact that no women were involved in the action, and wanted to make certain that at least one major star would be on hand as box-office insurance. Huston settled on Gregory Peck.

"Greg has colossal dignity and great masculinity," John says. "Yet he had never tackled anything like Ahab, which offers a substantial challenge to any actor. Melville's character is a complex man, at war with God. He sees the mask of the whale as the mask which the deity wears—and he sees the deity as a malignant being, out to torment the race of men as well as all other creatures. Captain Ahab is the world's dark champion who grapples with this enslaving force."

Playing Ahab, Peck would bear a long, jagged scar on his bearded face and stump about on a peg leg. His costumes would duplicate those worn by sea captains in the mid-1800s, and the ship he sailed would be authentic to the last detail.

Bradbury left for Europe that September on the S.S. *United States* with his wife and children. ("I finished reading *Moby Dick* at 4 A.M. one morning on the afterdeck in mid-Atlantic during a 100-mph hurricane—which I felt was most appropriate!") He met Huston in Paris, and they discussed Melville at the Longchamp track. In a letter to a friend, Bradbury wrote: "Huston says he is out to corrupt me; he looks forward to putting me on a horse, riding me to hounds, jetting me in a speedplane, and burying me in dope, drink and dames!"

Arriving in Dublin, where he would work at Courtown on the script, Ray was invited to walk the Irish countryside with Huston.

"It was a fine crisp afternoon, and we took off across the hills," says Bradbury. "As we were crossing an open field John spotted a huge black bull nearby, glowering at us. Before I could stop him, he'd whipped off his coat and was waving it like a bullfighter's cape in the brute's face, shouting, 'Ho-oh, *Toro*, ho-oh!' My God, I was paralyzed. Finally, the bull snorted, shook his head, and trotted away. John was actually disappointed because he hadn't charged!"

Huston's cast was truly international, a colorful group of professionals and amateurs gathered from many countries: Peck as Ahab; Britisher Leo Genn as Starbuck; Orson Welles as Father Mapple; the Dublin drama critic Seamus Kelly as Flask; Count Frederick Ledebur, the celebrated Austrian sportsman, as Queequeg; Edric Connor, a Calypso singer from Trinidad, as Daggoo. For a time, it seemed that John Godley, Lord Kilbracken, would portray the book's narrator, Ishmael, but Huston felt he needed an actor of experience for this key role, and eventually chose Richard Basehart.

The script kept Bradbury and Huston busy for six months, and proved extremely difficult, since the mystical essence of Melville had to be caught on the screen. Ahab's frenzied quest had many levels of meaning, and this film had to offer far more than the usual sea adventure.

"It was exhausting," says Bradbury. "I read the book at least nine times, and rewrote some of the scenes up to 30 times. In all, I did 1,500 pages to get a final 150. Through the early weeks in Ireland I found myself plagued with a vast depression. I felt that I had the weight, the burden of Melville on my back. When I gave Huston the first 60 pages I was ready to quit if he felt they were not right. But he liked what he read, and that gave me the confidence to continue."

They worked closely together scene by scene—with Huston shaping and correcting Bradbury's pages, scribbling changes in pencil, pacing as Ray typed, discussing and dissecting each line of dialogue.

"One of our big problems," says Huston, "was to turn Melville's expositional passages into characteristic dialogue. We decided at the outset that the picture was going to be as close to the original novel as we could possibly make it. But while the book had some tremendous action sequences, it had little actual plot. For screen purposes, we had to make some changes in Melville's construction—like transposing the scene in which Starbuck attempts to kill Ahab to the sequence that begins, 'It's a mild, mild day . . .' Or combining a number of scenes from the book into the one we call 'the chart scene' in which Ahab reveals to Starbuck his plan and purpose in following the white whale.

"Another major problem was putting into dialogue the basic

conflict between Starbuck and Ahab, the concept that a century ago whaling was actually considered a holy mission, bringing back oil for the lamps of the world. Starbuck registers shock and horror at Ahab's plan of vengeance against the whale as 'something unnatural.' Then, too, we had to get across the hypnotic effect Ahab exerts on his crew. He carried them to their doom, and it had to be logical that they would follow such a fanatic. Ray and I tried to be as faithful to the meaning of the novel as our own understanding and the special demands of the screen medium would allow."

Often when Bradbury worked at Courtown, Huston was out jumping Irish hedges.

"John had several bad falls," says Bradbury, "and would come limping in on canes. Every time he went out again, the rest of us at the house murmured a little prayer for his safety, because all of our jobs hung on that damned horse he was on."

The half-way point had been reached in the script when Huston came in one afternoon looking grave; he handed Bradbury a telegram which read: CANNOT PROCEED WITH FILM UNLESS SEXY FEMALE ROLE ADDED. It was signed: JACK WARNER.

"Has the man gone *insane?*" Bradbury shouted. "This is terrible! We can't stick a woman on board! My God, he can't be serious!"

Huston shook his head. "That's Hollywood, Ray. Warners is paying the bill, and if they want love interest we'll just have to get it in somehow. Maybe Ahab could have an affair with Gina Lollobrigida as a disguised stowaway . . ."

Furiously, Bradbury crumpled up the telegram and threw it to the floor; then he looked over at Huston.

"John was doubled up on the couch, laughing like a big monkey," he says. "That's when I knew *he'd* sent the thing. I was so relieved I couldn't get sore."

However, Bradbury managed to turn the tables neatly on a later occasion. "John had invited a group of 100% Lords and Ladies out to his Irish estate for dinner. He kept needling me to stay for the evening and I kept telling him I had nothing formal to wear. Well, he just kept needling me in front of Pete Viertel. Finally, when John had stepped out of the room, Pete hustled me upstairs. 'Let's show the bastard!' he chuckled, and dug up an old plaid skirt, some black leggings, a fringed purse, and a dinner jacket. 'Don't you see?' he asked, 'Kilts!' When the ultra-distinguished guests had arrived and John was in their midst playing the casual host, I came down the stairs. From the doorway, in a ringing voice, Pete announced me as 'Laird McBradbury.' All the Lords and Ladies turned in my direction. I saw Huston's jaw drop three feet; it was a lovely moment."

While the script moved slowly toward completion, Captain Ahab's ship was being just as painstakingly prepared.

The whaling vessel, Pequod, was graphically described by Melville in his novel, and Huston had his scouts ranging the seas through Norway, Holland and Denmark in an effort to find a similar craft. After a lengthy search for the wooden-hulled three-master, Huston's crew located a ship called the Rylands, floating off Scarborough, England. Launched nearly a hundred years ago, it had run cargo in the British Isles. When Huston purchased the ship it was serving as a tourist attraction, and housed a sea-going aquarium.

Art director Ralph Brinton and his team of experts set to work refitting the 104-foot craft to match Melville's Pequod. They stripped the Rylands down to her wooden hull and built a new deck some five feet above the old one, continuing the hull lines up to meet it. A new stern and transom were added, together with a quarter deck —and a false bow gave the ship the appearance of an early nineteenth century whaler. Five whaleboats were built to original specifications, along with a carpenter's bench and a try-works on the main deck (for boiling down whale blubber into oil).

For the ship's figurehead, special Obechi wood was obtained— and the head of an Indian from an extinct Massachusetts Pequod tribe was carved to Huston's satisfaction.

The Rylands had become the Pequod, a three-masted, square-rigged whaler, as tough and seaworthy as any ship of the line.

"We played a little trick on the viewer," says Brinton. "The crew of actors only *seem* to sail the Pequod. We had another wheel below decks connected to the real tiller. Six sailors, plus a boatswain, a mate and a skipper kept her from yawing or broaching to. You didn't see them on film, but they were there."

The false tiller, visible on the screen, was exactly as Melville had described it: made from the skull of a killer whale and the jawbone of a sperm whale.

Huston extended his mania for authenticity to the smallest details of dress and make-up.

"What a fiend he was for realism," says Peck. "We were all set on an old seafaring leg called a 'Chelsea peg' for Ahab. It has a cup into which the knee fits, with a wooden peg from there to the ground. But that didn't satisfy John. He pointed out that Ahab had lost the leg in the South Pacific and that Melville described the peg as being carved out of whalebone by the ship's carpenter. He wanted the one I wore to look as if it had been made at sea under rough conditions. He even showed me how to walk with it."

Frederick Ledebur was also forced to submit to Huston's realism, for it was Queequeg of whom Melville had written: "His chest and arms were checkered with the same squares as his face; his back too . . . and his legs were marked, as if a parcel of dark green frogs were running up the trunks of young palms. . . . For all his tattooings, he was on the whole a clean, comely-looking cannibal."

Huston had Ledebur's head completely shaved. Then a make-up man covered the actor's entire face and most of his body with an intricate Maori-like tattoo. Finally, a topknot of hair was fastened to Ledebur's bald head. (This process took over two hours each morning during the long months of shooting.)

Tensions were developing as the weeks passed.

In March of '54, with the main writing done, Bradbury and Huston clashed over a joke gone sour. They were due in England for final script work, and Huston (knowing Bradbury's fear of flight) told Ray that he'd reserved two seats for them on a night plane to London. Bradbury refused to be baited; he'd go by boat and train, and meet the director in London the next morning. Huston, suddenly angry, said this was ridiculous, but Bradbury was adamant. John's secretary was a friend of Ray's, and Huston threatened to cancel her vacation if Bradbury refused to fly with him. The two men exchanged heated words—and Huston took off for London, leaving Bradbury to his slower method of travel.

Huston was obviously under pressure; he'd been dreaming of bringing Melville to the screen for over a decade, and the mass of complex problems he now faced as producer-director were beginning to fray his nerves. He knew he had more to gain—or to lose—with *Moby Dick* than with any other film in which he had been involved.

Shooting was due to begin in July, and while Huston conferred with associates at the Elstree studios in London, his camera crew was off the Azores on a whaling expedition, gathering background action. And in Youghal, at the foot of the Knockmealdown Mountains on the estuary of the Blackwater, in County Cork, Huston's set workers were busily transforming this small Irish seaport village into a replica of New Bedford, Massachusetts. Power lines were removed, as well as all modern signs and street names; false fronts were built on the houses along the quayside; the dock was outfitted to duplicate New Bedford in 1840; the townspeople were dressed in costumes of the period. Even the harbor was deepened to accommodate Ahab's three-master.

Color was an equally important consideration, and Huston again worked with Oswald Morris, his director of photography on *Moulin Rouge*.

"I wanted the final print to have the strength found in steel engravings of sailing ships," says Huston. "Ozzie was able to give it to me."

Morris' main contribution was in the use of four negatives instead of the usual three. Over the color he superimposed a black-and-white negative, lending a hard, textured look to the print.

"This effect could never have been obtained by color alone," says Huston. "It required months of experimentation, because the balance between the negatives demanded infinitely precise adjustment.

"We also evolved a technique—for other scenes in the film—of muting the colors, giving us the grayed tones of a New England winter and the washed blues of sea weather. We'd deliberately pick overcast days in which to shoot such sequences, to heighten this effect."

By mid-April Bradbury had completed his final pages in London and was headed back for the States; his seven-month struggle with the White Whale had ended. Now it was Huston's job to bring the script to life—and for this the director had arranged a shooting schedule that would take *Moby Dick*'s crew half-way around the world.

Of the star players, Orson Welles had the smallest part, as a

New Bedford preacher. He appeared in just one sequence speaking from a pulpit shaped like the bow of a ship in a seacoast whaler's church, reading a sermon which recounts the story of Jonah and the whale. Yet this sermon, balanced against Ahab's obsession with *Moby Dick* as an Evil force, was vital—and Welles delivered his lines with fierce conviction.

The departure of the Pequod, filmed in revamped Youghal, featured the only women in the film. They stood gaunt and black against the sky, on high widows walks, waving goodbye to their sailing men—and Huston's camera work in this scene expertly set the mood for the sea adventures which lay ahead.

After shooting in Ireland Huston took the Pequod to Madeira, where Portuguese whalers still pursued the mammoths of the sea from open longboats.

"In a single day we killed 20 whales," says Huston. "Killed 'em the old way, with harpoons. This can be incredibly exciting—and unless you've harpooned a whale in a rough sea you haven't really hunted!"

The sea was a little rougher than Huston expected, and the giant model he was using for Moby Dick broke its towline and was soon lost among the waves. The RAF sent out search planes. Skippers were alerted throughout the area. The 92-foot monster weighed several tons due to the steel frame beneath its rubberized skin and posed a very real threat to small craft. (A second model broke away with Huston aboard, but was caught again before it could join its mechanical brother.)

While filming at sea Huston always managed to inject his own brand of horseplay into the day's activities—and one of his gags thoroughly startled the passengers on a passing steamer.

"John had everyone play dead on deck," says Basehart. "When the other ship passed us we were all sprawled about as if the hand of God had struck us down. It was really pretty funny."

On another occasion an actor's agent insisted on boarding the Pequod to watch the action. Annoyed, Huston told him where to stand, "so you won't get wet." He had been strategically placed by the director, and within moments a giant wave drenched him to the skin.

More problems arose with the costumes; they could not be kept dry on the Pequod's spray-washed decks—and an entire wicker factory in Ireland was put to work making 200 oversize wardrobe hampers, lined with canvas, for transportation at sea. The extra costumes were kept dry in these portable hampers. Also, Huston found that he needed some sperm-oil vats—and the Guinness' Stout brewery rushed 150 hogsheads to him from Dublin.

"There was always something to worry us," says Peck, who put in 27 exhausting weeks in place of his originally-scheduled 12. "When John told us he was going to shoot the Typhoon scenes right on the ship during an actual storm at sea we told him such a thing had never been done and that it was impossible. But it's a mistake to tell John that something is impossible. Then he's bound to do it."

In the script Ahab insists on keeping all sail flying while the storm rages—and this is the way Huston insisted on filming it.

"We began to think of John as a real-life Ahab," says Peck. "Three times we were sure we'd lost the Pequod—and three times she was de-masted. It's a miracle we survived."

Huston allowed salt water to break over the camera lens which he then dried with an air hose; he swung his cameras on elastic ropes in the wind—and shot footage on the tilting, storm-washed deck as his crew battled mountainous waves.

"Sure, we could have done most of it in a studio," Huston admits. "Yet there's nothing that compares with the fury of a real storm at sea. I wanted to capture as much of that on film as I could."

The waters off Fishguard, Wales, offered the next shooting site on Huston's agenda, and it was here that he worked with Lord Kilbracken on the script's final polish.

"I certainly never expected to be adapting Melville," says Kilbracken (who was still disappointed that he had not been able to land the part of Ishmael), "but John wanted some things done to the last third of the script and asked me to step in and help. I inserted three original scenes from Melville which pleased me—but working with Huston was something of a trial.

"On a Monday, for example, we would be precisely on the same wavelength, thinking in precisely the same way and fully understanding one another. On Tuesday, inexplicably, there would be no point of contact between us, and collaboration was impossible. On Wednesday he would suddenly speak with violent enthusiasm of what I had written—then the next day, tear the same scene to pieces. I was liable to be called any time from 7:30 in the morning to midnight. Working with Huston was exasperating, degrading and inspiring."

Costs rose swiftly on *Moby Dick*. The three-months planned location ran to eight, and damage to the Pequod, plus cast casualties, ate up time and money.

"There are always casualties on any picture John directs," says an associate who was working with Huston. "In this one Dick Basehart broke three bones in his foot jumping into a whaleboat; Leo Genn slipped a disc in his back and got pneumonia; Peck hurt his kneecap; a dozen men in the crew were injured at sea. And it could have been a lot worse."

In February of 1955, some 35 weeks after filming had begun, the final location shots were obtained in the Canary Islands—and Huston sailed the Pequod back to London.

Much remained to be done, particularly in the use of models representing the White Whale. In a gigantic concrete marine tank at the Elstree studios, made to hold several boatloads of harpooners, Ahab's enemy had been cunningly fashioned from latex and steel by Robert Clark, the British oceanographer and whale expert. Clark had divided his creation into three parts: head, tail and midsection. To cover these he used a mica-like plastic coated with white latex. A substance of aniline dye mixed with an oily chemical was added just beneath the false skin, and would "bleed" when harpooned. The three sections were mounted on metal frames in the 80,000-gallon tank, and activated by a special mechanism which allowed the beast to swim, leap, dive, chew up men and boats and shoot streams of water into the air. Smaller versions were also used in certain scenes. (In all, 20 electronic whales were constructed.)

Shooting the final scene, in which Moby Dick carries Ahab to a watery death, Huston arranged to have Peck lashed to the back of the huge mechanical beast so that he seemed caught there in a tangle of harpoon lines.

"By then I had a severe head cold," says Peck. "The wind machines were roaring and I was half drowned by torrents of water. Huston told me, 'I want you with your eyes staring open as you slowly come out of the sea on that whale's back—with your dead hand beckoning the men to their doom . . .' What I didn't know was that the winch they were using to rotate the section I was tied to was hand-operated. Later I learned that when they'd first tried it out the damn thing jammed! I could have *really* come up dead, which I think would have secretly pleased John—providing the last touch of realism he was after."

Before the edited print of *Moby Dick* was ready for viewing, costs had mounted to over $4,500,000. It had taken two years to film, but Huston was boyishly happy with the result. At the preview he kept exclaiming: "It's *good*, isn't it!"

The critics did not wholly agree. Reviews were mixed, and although most of them praised the film's color and technical brilliance, they faulted Huston for his selection of Gregory Peck.

"Peck's make-up for his role is expert," said Hollis Alpert, in the *Saturday Review*, "but the force needed for conviction is seldom present." And Eugene Archer elaborates: "Ahab, a role almost as difficult as Lear, is played by Gregory Peck in a deliberate, ranting style which . . . robs him of tragic stature. Huston's technique makes no apology for the actor's weakness, but places him as the focal point of the action in a manner which emphasizes the inadequacies of performance and crucially damages the center of the film . . . Peck struggles futilely with a role which demands the classical authority of a Ralph Richardson."

However, both critics found much to admire in the film, and Alpert stated: "Huston's re-creation of perhaps this most monumental of American novels is a kind of monumental work in itself." Archer comments: "If *Moby Dick* does not capture the full force of Melville, it conveys more depth than any American film of recent years. . . . It is probably as distinguished an adaptation of a great novel as the contemporary screen is capable of producing . . . a technical masterpiece, impressive in conception, formidable in execution—but emotionless at the core, a film for critics rather than patrons, difficult not to admire, impossible to enjoy."

Holiday magazine summed up: "*Moby Dick* is ultimately an intellectual achievement of considerable stature and power."

The Motion Picture National Board of Review cited Huston for "the year's best direction." He also won the New York Film Critics Award for Best Direction that same year with *Moby Dick*.

If he had not actually conquered the great White Whale, he had fought it with courage and high purpose. For Huston, the battle had been reward enough.

Chapter 12

FROM TIGERS TO TOBAGO

Hunting, like gambling, can become a drug—and those who are addicted to it are constantly seeking bigger, stronger, more danger-ous game. It is the dream of every hunter to bag a tiger—and to bring down a Bengal, largest of all tigers, is the ultimate in big-game thrills.

Early in 1956 John Huston had flown to India to scout loca-tions for a forthcoming film (Kipling's *The Man Who Would Be King*) on which he had been working with Peter Viertel. While there, Huston arranged to accompany two other hunters, Walter Buchen of Chicago and Felix Fenston of England, to Assam State, bordering the province of the Maharaja of Cooch Behar, where the biggest of the Bengals roamed. They journeyed from Calcutta to Assam's Camp Parbati, looking out on the rising foothills of the Himalayas. The camp was fully equipped and modern in most respects, with a spacious wooden dining room on stilts and a well stocked open-air bar.

The commanding officer of the hunt was Raj Kumar, and he told Huston and the others that the Bengal has a particular fondness for buffalo flesh; when a buffalo was attacked and eaten they would know that their quarry was within stalking range.

"A tiger generally kills before nightfall," explains Huston. "Having broken the neck of its prey, it licks a place raw with its sharp, scaly tongue and drinks blood. Thirsty from the salt, it seeks water. Then it finds some sheltered place in the jungle and rests till dawn, when it returns to finish its catch."

Each morning Huston would mount a ladder to the shooting platform of his howdah elephant and ride out to the hunt. He had selected a 12-gauge Rigby shotgun for smaller game and a twin-barreled .450 Holland & Holland for a try at the Bengals. A mahout rode astride the elephant's neck, tapping him with a hook for control.

"I potted a small hog deer that first day," says Huston, "but no tigers."

The second and third days were uneventful, but on the fourth morning a native came running in to inform the camp that his buffalo had been slain during the night; he would lead them to the spot where the killer cat lay in hiding.

"By 10 o'clock we were standing in our howdahs facing a green strip of thick jungle, guns at the ready. Felix was the only one of us who'd ever shot tiger, and we were a bit nervous, waiting it out. The beaters were working the brush, and we knew our elephants would instinctively sound the alarm when the tiger was due to appear.

"They suddenly began to trumpet—notes as pure and clear as any Louis Armstrong ever blew—and out he came, fast as a flaring bird. Felix fired twice. As I pulled the trigger, my elephant swayed wildly, throwing me to one side. I fired again, knowing I'd miss, as the yellow-and-black devil darted away into the brush. I figured later that he'd covered 200 yards in under 10 seconds—a good winner's time on a fast track!"

On the eighth morning, after a few days of calm, another Bengal appeared. Huston spotted it first, raising his rifle for a long 125-yard shot. A hit! The elephants were converging on the area when a warning cry made Huston and the others bring up their guns. A second tiger had been sighted.

"We heard the rattling, hollow, belching, infinitely hateful sound that is the growl of a Bengal," says Huston. "Then his stripes flashed, and he was in the open. Felix fired both barrels. Then I fired. But we'd missed. He was too quick for us."

The angry tiger was flushed out again by the beaters. Now it charged one of the trumpeting elephants, but Fenston's next shot brought it down. Huston's dead tiger measured out to eight and a half feet, and Fenston's to an even nine.

The hunt in India was over—and John Huston had bagged his Bengal.

"I returned to Ireland, switching from tigers to foxes," he says. "Riding to hounds offers equally as much action and excitement as stalking Bengals—and on any big hunt several people are thrown; you see them lying in ditches as you make your jump over them. That's the reason men wear scarlet coats and women wear black, so they'll show up clearly against the green turf when they fall."

Huston sent his wife to an Irish riding master, to improve her skill at the sport, but she didn't jump hedges with her husband's natural skill. "Once I saw Ricki flying out of the saddle and I thought: God, there goes the mother of my children! But she was lucky and only broke most of her lower teeth. I shipped her back to our dentist in the States for repairs and she was riding again in no time at all. After a really bad spill you have to get back on a horse the way a pilot has to fly again after a crash; otherwise you are likely to 'freeze' at a jump—which can be serious."

In October of 1955, during an interview with Louella Parsons, Huston revealed that he had just purchased St. Clerans, a 200-year-old stone mansion near Galway Bay in Craughwell, Ireland's western coastal region. "When I was a kid I never had a home," he told her. "I was always on the prod, living out of dressing rooms and hotels— so, all my life, I've been looking for the right place to settle. Now I've found it."

By the following year he'd made many improvements on the old Georgian structure. While restoring the stern face of the mansion, with hand-hewn blocks of gray granite, workmen uncovered several dozen human bones. The local constable declared them to be evidence of a recent mass murder—but when Huston checked with an archeologist and with historians in the area, he found that the bones belonged to members of a religious order who had lived on this site in the tenth century.

"The constable was quite let down," says Huston, "since he had counted on becoming world famous with his multiple-slaughter theory. Too bad. The Irish love a good murder."

The interior of St. Clerans became all-Huston; he refurnished the house completely, and with the help of Dublin architect Michael Scott created his own Shangri-La, a dazzling mixture of Old World luxury and New World comfort.

"St. Clerans will never be complete in my lifetime," he says, "because I bring items back from whatever new country I visit."

Here are posters by Lautrec, paintings by Monet and Utrillo and Juan Gris and Soutine, Louis XV mirrors, Chinese porcelains, Indian jade deities, African sculptures, heads from New Guinea, tile from Mexico, a French Gothic carved-wood Christ, bedspreads of rare silk, a seventeenth century bronze church chandelier, antique Spanish Colonial chairs, a Louis XIII refectory table, Aztec masks, baroque candelabra and a bed which once belonged to Napoleon.

Actor Peter O'Toole called it "Huston's Heaven"—and surely it approaches an earthly paradise, with its 100 acres of rich green grassland blending into the plains of Galway. The colonnaded courtyard is flanked by stone lions, and a central fountain tosses a bright spray into the Irish sky; the entry hall is lit with torches and its floor is of black marble. A moat surrounds the main yard, to keep Huston's animals—cows, sheep, horses, dogs—from trampling the formal gardens. Nearly every room has a giant fireplace, and there is an immense, sunken Japanese bathroom where guests may relax after a hunt. The director's priceless collection of pre-Columbian art is St. Clerans' star attraction, next to Huston himself. A staff of eight serve the family and maintain the grounds.

Facing the mansion, sitting merrily in the main courtyard, is a handsomely polychromed figure of the jester, Polichinelle, his iron head thrown back in mocking laughter.

"I found him rusting in the Paris Flea Market," says Huston. "You might say he represents the way I look at life."

During the period when he was editing *Moby Dick* the director planned to follow it with *Typee,* another Melville project starring Gregory Peck, which would be filmed in Tahiti and British Samoa. There was much talk of Huston's flying Peck to the islands in search of a beautiful native girl who would portray his wife—and a shooting date of July, 1956, had been tentatively assigned.

At the same time Huston talked of directing four 90-minute television spectaculars, including *Lysistrata,* with Marilyn Monroe, and *The Devil and Daniel Webster,* which his father had made as a motion picture. Then there was *The Man Who Would Be King* and *The Lark,* two other films Huston had in mind—along with the life story of his late photographer-friend, Robert Capa. He was also actively seeking rights to a play by Terence Rattigan, *The Sleeping Prince,* in which he hoped to pair up Marilyn Monroe and Sir Laurence Olivier.

None of these various projects materialized. Monroe herself obtained the rights to the Rattigan play; *Typee* proved too expensive; *King* had to be put off for more script work; the TV specials were abandoned.

"John was in debt way over his head," says an associate. "He owed thousands and needed a job from a major studio to pull himself out. That's the reason he took on *Heaven Knows, Mr. Allison*— because 20th offered him a fat three-picture contract he just couldn't afford to turn down."

That August John Huston celebrated his 50th birthday, vowing that he would live to be 100. When a reporter asked him how he could be so sure, Huston grinned. "Son," he said, "when you go to bed at night all you have to do is promise yourself a shot glass of bourbon first thing in the morning. That way, you've got something to wake up to."

When 20th Century-Fox signed Huston they turned over a controversial property to him. *Heaven Knows, Mr. Allison* was originally a novel by Charles Shaw. Producer Eugene Frenke had purchased screen rights late in 1952 for director William Wyler. The World War II theme of a nun and a marine trapped together by the Japanese on an island in the South Pacific was difficult to handle, since powerful church authorities stated that they would ban such a film. In 1954 Wyler submitted a treatment in which the girl revealed that she was not really a nun, but had stolen a nun's clothing in the hope of escaping in disquise. This story line won church sanction, but Wyler moved to other projects and *Allison* was put on the shelf. It was reactivated for Huston.

"In our version the girl had not taken her final vows," said Huston. "Even so, we kept away from any implication of sex. I did the script with John Lee Mahin, and there was nothing censorable anywhere in it."

The spot Huston had chosen to film the story was called Tobago, a British colony approximately 20 miles off Trinidad at the southern limit of the Caribbean. (He'd chosen Tobago because it closely resembled an island in the South Pacific, and was a place where he could spend the studio's money in pounds sterling for this "British quota" picture.)

Robert Mitchum and Deborah Kerr agreed to star as the American marine and the Irish nun; the only other speaking roles in the film would be Japanese.

"We needed eight Japanese who could speak their native tongue fluently," says Huston. "They really didn't have much to do —just talk casually to one another for a scene in the officers' mess— but finding them was not easy. It *should* have been, but it wasn't."

"The search for those eight Japanese took us two months. It was fantastic!" says a Huston aide. "There was not a single bona fide Japanese in the whole Caribbean—and we ranged as far south as Brazil. Finally got our eight in San Paulo. The other 'Japanese' in the film were really Chinese. We imported them from Trinidad, along with a hundred U.S. marines, for the beach fighting stuff."

Fishermen in that area were alerted to be on the lookout for giant turtles, as Huston needed a king-sized one to tow Mitchum for an underwater sequence.

"They found a huge son of a gun," says Mitchum. "Must have been at least 300 pounds. In the story I was supposed to catch him for food. Well, he towed me underwater for what seemed like miles. Almost dragged me into a coral reef. I saw the reef in time, otherwise that turtle might have ended up dining off me instead of the other way around."

Shooting began in September and had been in progress for a month when Huston received a cable from producer David Selznick. He wanted Huston to direct the Ben Hecht screenplay on Hemingway's *A Farewell to Arms*, and would pay $250,000 for the job. Happily, John accepted. Fox would grant him a release for the Selznick production after he had completed *Allison*. The deal was set, and Huston expressed his satisfaction at being able to direct a major Hemingway property.

For the village scenes on Tobago, natives had constructed several thatch-roofed houses, a small church and a bamboo filming tower. Explosive charges were placed among the houses and the church for the bombing sequence, and Huston invited visiting film critic Hollis Alpert to watch the action. They climbed to the top of the bamboo tower, where Huston carefully explained that unless the charges were timed to a split-second the actors in the scene would be caught inside the range of the explosion.

"It's set to go off at the count of 10 after I give the signal," said Huston. "Are you ready, kid?"

Alpert said he was, but looked nervous.

"Okay, here goes." Huston raised a hand to start the action. Then, tensely, he began the count: "One . . . two . . . three . . . four . . . five . . ."

A huge explosion rocked the tower; the village erupted in smoke and flame.

Huston shook his head. "Timing was off," he said darkly.

Alpert reeled back. "Oh, my God! Those *men* . . .They must be—"

The director climbed down, concealing his grin. Naturally, there was no accident; Huston's intention had been to shock Alpert—and the stunned critic didn't find out that the actors were safe until he reached the ground.

However, the joke became reality in a later explosion, when one of Huston's special effects men was nearly blinded by a delayed charge.

Mitchum also suffered making *Allison*. He wrenched an ankle in a battle sequence and sustained a deep cut on one of his feet. Then, sliding down a palm tree, he took several layers of skin off his chest. Mitchum's attitude through all this was placid: "You work for John, you suffer. What else can you expect?"

Huston praised the actor: "Bob is a wonderful guy . . . amusing, intellectual . . . very much in the Bogart mold."

When the director was informed that an official studio representative was headed for Tobago in order to check out any remaining elements in the script which might prove censorable Huston immediately set up a scene for him to witness.

"We've added this new sequence to the film," Huston told the man upon his arrival. "Thought you'd enjoy watching us shoot it."

The censor seemed pleased at the opportunity, but as the sequence progressed he began to turn pale. "Great Scott!" he whispered to Huston. "Mr. Mitchum is *seducing* the nun! This is absolutely horrible! You can't allow—" Huston told him to be quiet, that it was too late now to make any further script changes.

What the sweating censor didn't know was that Huston was directing the scene behind an empty camera.

In all, the crew of *Heaven Knows, Mr. Allison* spent four months on location.

"Got myself a good heavyweight in Tobago," says Huston. "Named Ervin Allen. Sent him to England to train. I always like to keep some money tied up in a good fighter."

Although Huston and Mahin were nominated by the Academy for Best Screenplay, most critics found *Heaven Knows, Mr. Allison* pleasant but undistinguished. *Films and Filming* said: "Cinemascope and censorship effectively destroyed its chances for distinction. The film is nonetheless good entertainment, technically competent, and perceptive in the characterizations of Mitchum and Deborah Kerr."

Huston returned to Hollywood early in 1957—to find his old friend Bogie critically ill with cancer. On January 14 the actor died, and a shaken Huston delivered the public oration. Eight hundred mourners crowded into the All Saints Episcopal Church in Beverly Hills for Bogart's funeral. And while it was in progress the actor's remains were cremated at Forest Lawn.

Huston spoke of Bogie's great hospitality, which had endured to the last days. "He fed a guest's spirit as well as his body," the director said. "He would ply you with good will until you became drunk in the heart as well as in the legs . . ."

On the altar was a scale model of Bogart's beloved yacht, the Santana.

Preparations for *A Farewell to Arms* were moving into their final stages, and Huston had discussed the project with Hemingway in Paris before returning to the States. Papa liked his ideas, recalling Huston's script on *The Killers,* and both men felt the book could make a powerful film.

Farewell marked David O. Selznick's return to picture-making after almost a decade. The producer of *Gone With the Wind* had not made a film since *Portrait of Jenny* in 1948, and he was extremely concerned about the potential of this Hemingway property.

From the outset, Seznick worried about Huston; he felt that the director was not going to take orders gracefully. Within a month after they began working together Selznick and Huston clashed over Ben Hecht's script. Huston wanted more of Hemingway in; Selznick didn't. The storm was building. . . .

During a David Selznick picture memos flooded out to every department from the producer, who dictated them at night in relays to three secretaries.

"David would never dictate less than 50 a night," claims a Selznick aide. "The total might reach 100 before dawn—and a single memo could run to 25 typed pages. Only Jerry Wald was in the same class with David when it came to memos."

Shooting was set to begin during late March, in Italy, and Huston worked with Hecht on final script revisions, then left for Europe. A Selznick memo followed him, canceling many of the revisions he'd made. The storm had broken. . . .

On March 20, three days before the cameras were due to roll, Huston arrived on location in Italy with the script he and Hecht had been revising for two months. In his hotel room at Cortina d'Ampezzo Huston found a new script—from Cesare Zavattini and two other Italian writers—which Selznick had ordered as being "more commercial." A 16-page memo accompanied the script.

In this long memo Selznick told Huston that he was "desperately unhappy" with the state of the picture, saying that he was prepared to throw out Hemingway's book, having "wrung it dry," and that he expected Huston to function under his terms as he outlined them. Otherwise, John was free to resign and another director would be brought in.

Huston resigned, stating that he could not possibly function under such conditions.

Selznick told the press: "In Mr. Huston, I asked for a first violinist and instead I got a soloist . . . As the producer, mine must be the final word. I have signed Charles Vidor to direct my film."

As finally produced—with Selznick's wife, Jennifer Jones, as the nurse and Rock Hudson as the soldier—*A Farewell to Arms* emerged as a dull, dismal film.

Art Buchwald, who was in Europe during this period, reports: "John sure wasn't the *only* one to resign. A chief of photography, three art directors, a film editor, a special effects director, four chauffeurs and the entire staff of Selznick's villa in Italy all walked out. They must have been driven memo-mad—because, by the time the picture was over, Selznick had dictated 10,000 memos!"

Huston had no further comment to make regarding *Farewell;* he was already fighting the problems of his next film, which would be shot entirely in Japan.

Chapter 13

A BARBARIAN IN JAPAN

In the centuries before Admiral Perry opened Japan to Western trade at gunpoint the country existed as a feudal empire, savagely ruled by the sword. Japanese warlords were all-powerful. They valued their isolation, and foreigners who landed on their shores were tortured and beheaded.

The first American diplomat to enter this forbidden area was Townsend Harris, appointed consul general to Japan in 1855. A devout Christian, Harris never touched liquor and stoutly refused to work on Sundays. It was his duty to negotiate a treaty with Japan on behalf of the United States—thus opening up a trade link between the two countries. While in Japan, Harris hired a young washing woman to maintain his quarters. On her second visit he noted that the girl had a skin infection, and fired her immediately. From this brief association, Japanese legends flowered—concerning a love affair between a beautiful geisha and her "barbarian" from the West. In truth, Harris would never have condoned such immoral conduct, did not like Japanese women, and died a bachelor at 73. Yet legend outweighed fact, and the strait-laced diplomat became a romantic folk hero.

In 1957 John Huston decided to film the legend of Townsend Harris as his second production for 20th Century-Fox.

"If I have one heritage from my father," he said to reporters, "it is respect for the source; Dad told me to go to life itself for my material. Well, after I saw *Rashomon* and *Gate of Hell* I wanted to make a Japanese picture. Not an American picture in Japan. No. A real, honest-to-God Japanese picture using Japanese crews, shot over there from first frame to last. And now that I have the right property I'm going to go make it. I'm going to the source."

Who would play Harris? Huston grinned, lighting a long brown cigar.

"Only one man is right for him—and that's John Wayne. I want to send Duke's gigantic form into the exotic world that was the Japanese empire in the 1800s. Imagine!—this massive figure, with his bluff innocence and naivete, with his edges rough, moving among these minute people. Who better to symbolize the big, awkward United States of 100 years ago? Duke's our man."

Wayne didn't come cheap. In fact, when the contracts were drawn, he was guaranteed the highest salary any actor had been paid up to that time: nearly $700,000—for working a period of 14 weeks.

Charles Grayson would do the script, in which Harris becomes involved with Okichi, a lovely young geisha, is spied upon and attacked by a combative samurai, becomes the enemy of the governor of Shimoda, and burns down a Japanese village to combat a cholera epidemic. Very little of the real Harris would appear on the screen; he was far too tame and unromantic for Huston.

Originally titled *The Townsend Harris Story*, the film would be shot mainly at Kyoto, Japan's "cultural capital," spared in the war by MacArthur and containing over 800 temples and shrines, many of them ancient. For the opening scenes of the Harris landing, and for the fire sequence, Huston had chosen Kawana, a fishing village some 200 miles to the east. Interiors would be shot at the Kyoto Eiga studio.

"Finding our legendary geisha took some doing," says Huston.

Tony Huston, John's 13-year-old son, becomes
an actor in THE LIST OF ADRIAN MESSENGER, which
was filmed near Huston's castle in Ireland.

Huston, riding to hounds in full gear, takes on an Irish hedge.

As Cardinal Glennon
of Boston in
Otto Preminger's
THE CARDINAL.

Sharing a joke with Richard Burton and Liz Taylor
in Mexico, for THE NIGHT OF THE IGUANA.

Keeping cool in Mismaloya.

Parrot and friend.

Huston directs "Eve" in the Garden of Eden sequence from THE BIBLE, with "Adam" in foreground.

In front of the huge Times Square sign advertising
THE BIBLE, with the film's producer, Dino De Laurentiis.

Alone with his problems, John Huston ponders the future.

"We were shown film on 150 Japanese actresses—and actually tested 29, but we couldn't locate the type we needed."

Visiting a geisha house, Huston discovered a lovely 17-year-old apprentice. The house mother agreed to let him give her a screen test, but only if he'd pay the girl $1,200 "pillow money" in advance. Huston agreed to these terms, but the test was never made. "The poor dear got appendicitis," says Huston. "So we had to keep on looking."

Huston's next stop was the Nichigeki Music Hall, and there he watched a singing stripper known as "The Tokyo Venus." Her name was Eiko Ando, and she had never appeared professionally beyond the limits of a burlesque stage.

"I knew she was our gal," says Huston. "For one thing, she was tall for a Japanese—five foot seven—which would help in the scenes with Wayne, who's six foot four. Additionally, she possessed a lovely, low-pitched voice and moved with a dancer's natural grace. Of course she couldn't speak a word of English."

In working with her, Huston used an interpreter, taking great pains to instruct the girl in every movement and inflection. Also, she had never worn the traditional kimono—and had to be taught to act and walk in the manner of a geisha.

Completing the main cast was one of Huston's oldest friends, Sam Jaffe, as Heusken, the interpreter who worked with Harris in effecting the treaty. Jaffe survived a fall from the saddle during a parade sequence when a pole from a Japanese sedan-chair passed between his leg and the side of the mount he was riding. The incident amused Huston: "I'd say Sam was the victim of the first accident between a horse and a sedan-chair in the past hundred years."

In his strong desire to capture the true flavor of early-day Japan on film Huston hired several top Japanese technicians and obtained the services of three of the country's finest directors. One of them, Teinosuke Kinugasa (responsible for *Gate of Hell*, which had first inspired Huston to consider a film in the Orient), became script supervisor.

"We really didn't have the script in any kind of finished form," says Charles Grayson. "In fact, for a while there, it was touch and go as to whether I'd have a scene done by the time John wanted to film it."

Two other writers, Alfred Hayes and Nigel Balchin, also worked on the Harris story—keeping just ahead of Huston's shooting schedule.

A minor crisis arose over the title of the picture. Huston was setting up for a take beside an 1,100-year-old Buddhist temple when Grayson handed him a clipping from a Hollywood trade paper. "*Townsend Harris Story* change," it read. "Final title, announced by Fox, is *The Barbarian and the Geisha.*"

Huston became enraged—and sent a telegram to Fox executive Buddy Adler declaring that he'd withdraw his name from the finished film if it bore the "ridiculous" new title. Eugene Frenke, who was producing the picture in Japan with Huston, eventually talked him out of this decision. "I *like* it," Frenke told him. "After all, John, we do have a barbarian and we do have a geisha. It makes sense."

(Huston got his revenge on Frenke by assigning him a bit part as a splendidly-dressed Japanese soldier, then seeing to it that he got dumped head first into a lake while wearing his full uniform.)

Thus, the new title became official.

On many levels, Wayne and Huston were basically incompatible—and their relationship began to go sour when the Duke told Huston that John Ford was a close friend and that the director would appreciate anything Huston could do for Wayne. "For example, my best profile is on the right." Huston said that was dandy—and aimed his camera, whenever possible, at the left side of Wayne's face.

After the actor had looked over rushes on the early scenes he was quoted as saying: "I don't see anything in this picture so far that suits me. Huston has me walking through a series of Japanese pastels. Hell, my fans expect me to be tall in the saddle . . . and I must be a whole foot shorter from bumping my head on these little doors. . . .

"Usually I gain a director's confidence, but when I go up to Huston's room and ask what's coming up for the day he sighs and points out the window. 'Duke, just look at that view. Isn't it magnificent?' . . . For a while I couldn't make up my mind whether to flat quit and go home and let them sue me or stay on and give this thing a whirl. Guess I'm in so deep now I can't back out—but ole Duke's not happy, I tell you that."

When a hotel clerk failed to show up with his key one night

Wayne made his own entrance by hurling his full 220 pounds through the wall.

His fight scene in *Barbarian* saw him pitted against a tiny Judo expert who tossed around the giant actor as easily as a child tosses a ball. Wayne kept muttering darkly about what his fans would think during this battle, but Huston was delighted with the footage.

Added to Wayne's troubles: a forced landing six miles at sea in a plane with engine failure—and a minor eye operation, performed on the set.

"In Kawana, they wanted to bounce me from my hotel," says Wayne, "to make space for their weekend regulars. But I held out."

The actor told the management that he was in bed with a cold and would die if removed from his rooms. Later, at another demand to evacuate, he said he'd have to be *carried* from his quarters. Reduced to a single room in the suite, he threatened to burn down the hotel if ejected. (Ironically, two weeks after Wayne's departure, the hotel actually *did* burn down.)

The film's production manager, William Eckhardt, was responsible for all hotel accommodations—and he had 256 people staying in 42 different hotels scattered over the location area. Actually, some of the "hotels" were houses of ill fame, a fact which Huston kept from waiting Stateside wives. ("They simply would not have understood our space problem.")

Another problem for Eckhardt presented itself when he was told to round up 32,000 bunches of artificial cherry blossoms. (The blossoms would be tied to bare December branches in order to simulate a spring climate.) Eckhardt calmly put a Japanese manufacturing house to work on the order.

However, Eckhardt's coolness under pressure vanished utterly during an incident concerning a Japanese technician. It seems that the man had been accused by Eckhardt of dishonesty. The next morning the technician walked up to Eckhardt and presented him with a small wooden box. When the production manager opened it he gasped in shock. Inside the box, resting on a tiny velvet cushion, was the severed little finger from the technician's left hand. In Japan, a man's honor is worth more than his finger.

Charles Clarke was behind *Barbarian's* color camera, and Huston worked closely with him in capturing the delicate tints and shadings he wanted on film. The beauty of Japan had overwhelmed Huston, and he wished to make certain it reached the cinema public.

"We got some great stuff," he says. "We shot in the Temple of Flowers, at Nijojo Castle and at shrines all over Kyoto. I found treasures to use as props. We had one set in which not an object in it was less than 300 years old! I was able to dress an actress in clothing that an empress had worn—and I brought back a lovely Japanese screen which was a steal at $1,700.

"There's a doll maker in Kyoto, and when he is working on a doll he waits until 3 o'clock in the morning to paint the eyes; he waits until the world is quiet and serene—and he captures this wonderful serenity in the eyes of his dolls. Now, if a man could capture that on film . . ."

The interior set for the Shogun's palace, where Wayne would present his treaty, covered 12,000 square feet, and no soundstage in Japan was large enough to house it; the set was finally built in Kyoto's Exhibition Hall, requiring special soundproofing and electrical equipment.

In working at the Hanano Tera location, near Kyoto, Huston found his view blocked by a gnarled old cherry tree. He found the abbot of the temple, to whom the tree belonged, and told him he would have it uprooted, shoot his scene, then plant a new tree in its place. Was that all right?

"No, my son," the wrinkled abbot said. "This noble tree still clings to life. Through the years it has bloomed here, bringing beauty to the hearts of generations. It is not for us, my son, to decide that its usefulness has ended."

Huston nodded solemnly. "It shall be given a place of honor in my film," he assured the abbot.

And, indeed, the old tree became the center of Huston's scene.

An adaptable director, Huston often utilized the unexpected while making *Barbarian*. When a small Japanese boy laughed at Wayne as the actor walked past him during a scene Huston decided not to re-shoot. ("If that kid thinks he looks funny today, then a kid of 100 years ago would have thought so too.") Similarly, as a little girl began to cry during a subsequent scene her tears became part of the action. And when an intricate shadow-pattern cast by several actors caught Huston's attention he shot the shadows instead of the actors.

A prime example of extemporaneous filming in *Barbarian* is the big dolphin-killing sequence. At Kawana, Huston had hired some 350 fishermen for background footage and had dressed them in costumes of the period. One morning the men became highly agitated. They leaped into their sampans and headed for open sea—having sighted a school of dolphin out beyond the breakwater.

It took the fishermen three days to herd the dolphin into shore and slaughter them, with Huston filming the sequence.

"I figured I might as well," he said. "They were going fishing, and the devil take our movie! As it was, it cost us about 25 grand in lost time for them to chase those fish."

Eckhardt also had to pay 276 fishermen to keep their modern boats out of the harbor—and he estimated the cash outlay on *Barbarian* had by then risen to $55,000 per day.

"It ended up costing over three and a half million," he says. "This was the first period production ever attempted by Americans, and was the costliest movie ever made in Japan. Up to 900 people were used in a single bit of action."

Almost a million dollars of the studio's money went to Huston and Wayne (with the director getting $300,000 for his services). The Duke recalled what he had been paid the first time he ever worked for 20th: "That was in '29—and I got 75 bucks a week."

For a harbor shot, Huston needed a four-masted cadet training vessel, and he talked the Japanese Maritime Defense Board into letting him use it. However, the captain was a stubborn man who refused to unfurl his sails.

"Take me out to the ship," said Huston. "I'll talk to him."

No, the captain told Huston when he stepped on board, the sails must remain furled. John asked if he might share some tea with the captain, knowing he would not be refused. Below deck, Huston spotted a 12-volume set of the sailing works of Alan Villiers.

"Ah, I see you read Alan's work," Huston mused, idly turning the pages of a volume.

The captain's face radiated sudden interest. "Indeed, yes— do you *know* him?"

"He's a warm, dear, close and valued friend," declared the director.

As Huston left the ship the captain was bowing and smiling—and the sails were unfurled.

John Huston is a man seldom given to serious self-doubts, but with *Barbarian* he felt that the production had somehow gotten away from him, that he had over-extended himself. To Frenke, he confessed: "Sometimes I wake up in the night, terrorized by the thought that all the bits and pieces I've shot cannot be made to fit into an integrated whole—that I have finally painted my way into a corner."

Frenke assured him that things were not all that bad.

"What worries me, John, is the fire stuff. We could get into real trouble with the fire stuff."

Frenke was referring to the sequence in which Wayne puts a torch to a village infected with cholera for the purpose of halting an epidemic. The set had been constructed on a headland close to a series of ancient Japanese buildings, and if the flames got out of control they could ignite the whole town.

Kawana, on the jagged coastline of the scenic Izu Peninsula, some 72 miles southwest of Tokyo, was the site chosen for the fire —and it had already served as the port at which Harris disembarks when he first arrives in Japan. The earlier sequence had been exceedingly difficult to arrange, since all surface evidence of the modern age had to be erased. Thatched rice straw was stacked over tin roofs; telephone wires were re-routed; cables were taken down and run through underground conduits; a 14-foot TV antenna had to be dismantled.

"It was Youghal all over again," says Huston.

The real port of Shimoda where Harris landed (40 miles down-coast) on September 4, 1856, was much too modern for Huston to use.

Now Kawana was doing double-duty for the cholera scenes—but as the fire-fighting equipment was readied, and final preparations were made to record Wayne's mission of mercy, Huston paced nervously behind the camera. He was not satisfied with the scene as written.

"Why would they let Harris live if he tried a stunt like this?"

Huston asked Grayson. "Why wouldn't they just chop the bastard?"

The writer looked worried. "Maybe the governor allows him to live so that he will have a good excuse to arrest Harris and ship him back to America as a criminal. How does that sound?"

Huston told him to go write the scene that way.

"While you wait?"

"While I wait," snapped the director.

Grayson rushed off to write the new scene. When he returned, Huston read the pages, nodded, made a few deletions, then gave them to the script girl to have duplicated.

"Okay, let's shoot it," he said.

Duke Wayne complained that an important line had been lost in the revision; Huston said fine, to go ahead and speak the line. Everyone looked tense.

The action finally got underway; Wayne and Jaffe moved among the houses, putting each one to the torch. Extras scampered about in mock-terror. The governor and his samurai appeared on cue, shouting their new lines. The two Americans were accused of a criminal action and hauled off by the samurai after an angry exchange of dialogue.

"The entire set was an inferno," reports Grayson. "The only spot still clear of the holocaust was the area where the governor arrested Wayne. And even it was being seriously threatened by the spreading fire. John ordered another take on the dialogue scene: 'Again, from the governor's entrance!' The scene was repeated as things grew hotter. 'Again!' yelled John—and the sweating actors obeyed. 'Once more!' John commanded. This third take was it; Huston had what he wanted."

By this time Jaffe's pants were smoking, and Wayne had scorched one arm and burned his thigh. A first-aid man rushed toward them.

"I think we got some good fire stuff," grinned Huston.

For the last day's shooting a 40-foot barge, filled with kerosene, was scheduled to burn and explode in a fiery climax to the cholera sequence. All went as planned until a safety cable broke and the flaming barge drifted in among the moored sampans of the fishermen.

"I could envision the whole town going up in smoke," says Huston.

In an unscheduled bit of heroics Wayne sprinted across the wharf and led the film crew in a successful effort to extinguish the flames before the barge exploded. Then a full-scale fist fight broke out between the angry fishermen and the crew.

"Boy, that fight was a beaut," recalls Huston. "Too bad we couldn't have used it in the picture."

By February of 1958, after three months on location in the Orient, Huston was back in Hollywood to help edit and score his footage. But discussions with 20th Century-Fox officials turned bitter, and Huston left the film to studio hands for completion.

Wayne and Huston were no longer on speaking terms. When reporters pressed the director for details he smiled crookedly. "Suppose you just say that there is no great meeting of souls."

Reviewers tended to support Wayne's sour opinion of *The Barbarian and the Geisha*. Even the industry trade papers noted that "it has little of the action the public expects in a John Wayne picture."

Newsweek hated Wayne and called the film "lamentably tedious." The *Saturday Review* was more complimentary: "This is an unusually beautiful film, directed with spirit and remarkable taste by John Huston, absolutely undaunted by his uninspiring plot material." The *New Yorker* acidly observed: "We are offered some fine views of Japan. Maybe Mr. Huston should have settled for a travelogue." And another critic noted that "while the film is continuously pleasing to the eye, it seldom stirs the mind or touches the heart."

Time had the final word: "Ouch—there goes three million bucks!"

Two weeks after his arrival in California Huston boarded a plane for another adventure; he was headed for the searing barrens beyond the Hill of the Demons in the savage French Cameroons.

Chapter 14

FROM ELEPHANTS TO INDIANS

In French Equatorial Africa the killing temperatures range up to 140 by day, from 90 to 100 by night. The sun is a blast furnace in the raw, blistered sky. Liquids are sweated out before they can reach the interior of the body. Malaria is king. The roads are the most primitive in the world. It is a literal hell on earth.

This was the locale picked by Huston for his next film.

"It's elephant country," he had told the press. "The book we're going to make concerns wild elephants—we'll go find some in French Africa."

The book was Romain Gary's *The Roots of Heaven*—which had won the coveted Prix Goncourt in France. It tells the story of Morel, a man frantically driven by a desire to stop the slaughter of elephants before the great herds become extinct. He rallies the natives to do battle with ivory hunters. "These beasts are the last free things on earth," says Morel. "They *must* be preserved."

William Holden was set to star, but pulled out at the last moment. Trevor Howard took his place, backed by a cast which included Errol Flynn, Juliette Greco, Eddie Albert and Orson Welles.

"I read the book and liked it," declares Huston. "So I asked the studio to buy it for me—but Darryl Zanuck exercised his option with Fox to pick his own subject every two years and chose *Roots* for himself. Now, I was a little hesitant about working closely with another strong-minded producer—after all the Selznick memoranda —but we talked things over and agreed to try this together. I wanted very much to direct the picture."

Welles would do his bit in Paris, at the Boulogne Studio after location shooting, but the rest of the cast accompanied Huston and Zanuck (and a vast army of American, French, Italian and English technicians and set workers) into the depths of Africa.

"Everybody got sick on this one," says Huston. "It was the roughest location I'd ever attempted."

The African heat was so intense that Huston was unable to maintain a normal shooting schedule. He would begin at dawn, shoot until noon, then be forced to quit for the day. (The film stock had to be stored in iced containers.) Even with these precautions Eddie Albert collapsed from sunstroke, soon becoming delirious.

"Eddie was out of his head for a couple of days," Huston says. "But he survived okay."

Others were not as fortunate. Malaria and amoebic dysentery took a severe toll of cast and crew. One Italian who had neglected to swallow his anti-malaria pills contracted the most virulent form of the disease and died. Zanuck's son-in-law, young Bobby Jacks, also came down with this form of malaria, but rallied after medical treatment.

In all, there were 960 sick calls, embracing everything from sore toes to gonorrhea, and many members of the troupe had to be shipped back to their homes. One poor fellow was sent to Paris with an ailment so obscure that not even the Pasteur Institute could identify it.

Errol Flynn claimed an immunity to African illness. "I've been through the jungles of New Guinea," he said. "They were enough to prepare me for anything. Also, I refuse to drink water on location, sticking with vodka and fruit juice—which no doubt helps."

Huston related a humorous but horrifying incident with regard to alcohol vs. Africa: "Three of us went to call on one of the local governors here in Africa, and were very cordially received. We'd brought along some Scotch and when we offered this to the governor he insisted that we drink from his personal stock. It was dark by the end of our visit, and a long way back to camp, so we asked if we might be put up for the night. He said it would be his pleasure— and turned us over to a young native with a lantern, who led us out into the jungle.

"We must have walked for half an hour. Then the boy stopped in front of a small hut, gestured us inside, and left the lamp. We looked around. No furniture, no beds, just an old automobile seat with horsehair sticking out in twenty places! No window panes, just bars. We figured it must have once been used as a native jail. When we turned to tell the boy that we certainly couldn't spend the night here he had vanished. We had no idea how to find our way back to the governor's house.

"One guy took the auto seat, and the other two of us decided to sit it out till morning, playing cards, since it was impossible to sleep on that floor. Then the insects started flying in, drawn by the lamplight. Swarmed all over us, and bit like hell. So we broke open our Scotch and began slugging it down as fast as we could. After a while we didn't notice the insects so much. A while longer and we didn't notice them at *all*.

"By morning the guy on the auto seat was so badly bitten he had to spend two weeks in the hospital. We were in pretty good shape, thanks to the Scotch. I guess bugs don't get as much fun out of biting a drunk. At least that's been my experience."

Flynn, who did not use a double in the film, was required to perform a number of dangerous stunts—one of which called for him to navigate a stream at Port Archambeau clinging to the tail of his horse. In mid-stream Flynn heard pistol shots; several gregarious crocodiles were being discouraged from joining the actor.

"John, you son of a bitch!" shouted Flynn. "Get me out of this stinking river before one of these bastards has me for lunch!"

Huston smiled sympathetically—then called for another take. (After the footage was in the can, Flynn was informed that a week earlier a French officer had been seized by a big crocodile just three hundred yards upshore.)

Yet Huston and Flynn were of a stripe; they shared the same rebellious attitude toward life, combined with a wild love for the exotic which made them brothers. Between scenes they formed a private hunting safari.

In writing of it, Flynn said: "We saw everything . . . great surges of elephants, weirdly-colored birds, the rare giant eland, and the water buffalo—said to be the most dangerous of all African beasts. Huston got one of the largest pairs of horns for a trophy, and was like a kid with his first lollipop. . . . He was obviously very good in the bush. I thought I was pretty good, but ole Johnny leaped along through the jungle like a big spider. He was hard to keep up with."

Half-French, half-Corsican Juliette Greco (who once worked as a lady bouncer in a Left Bank bistro) had the only feminine role in *Roots* and was not too happy over this fact.

"I am only woman sleeping with *many* men," she said in her broken English. "Men are snoring plenty and I am not liking that too much. We are all in big hut, and in morning these men are waking up, some very nicely, some not so nice. Mr. Trevor Howard always waking up nice, but Mr. Huston not always waking up so nice."

Huston's direction was frustrating to Miss Greco. "He never say I am good or I am bad. First, I think he must hate me. Then he look at me like a snake with little, slitted eyes, and he say through his teeth, 'Fine, honey, fine.' Then I know he like me."

The Lake Tchad area in French Equatorial Africa had previously been explored only by daredevil adventurers with 16-mm cameras. Huston's most fortunate moment during the exhausting months of location was in accidentally coming upon a vast herd of 600 wild elephants at dawn on the banks of an African river. "We got some fabulous color footage on that herd," says Huston. "Ozzie Morris was with me again on *Roots* as my chief cameraman and we both knew we'd really lucked into something. You don't bump into 600 elephants every day in the week—not even in Africa!"

Huston was fighting time; there had been many delays with equipment—and the widespread sickness among his crew had also slowed production. In July, as John pointed out, "the whole sky caves in." The heavy, unrelenting seasonal rains could be disastrous, rendering the already-poor roads completely impassable. Time was therefore critical.

"We barely made it," says Trevor Howard. "Huston got us out of there just half a day ahead of the rains. Twelve more hours in Africa —and we might all be there yet!"

Zanuck, who had withstood the rigors of location, came down with a case of the shingles upon the unit's return to Paris. Flynn suffered a touch of malaria (despite his vodka and juices) and entered a French hospital for a rest. Juliette Greco was found to have contracted a rare disease of the blood in which her white corpuscles far outnumbered the red. Her blood pressure had fallen dangerously low.

Huston, of course, was in perfect health.

The Boulogne Studio housed the film's interior sets, and Huston appeared there in typical garb. One day he would be wearing a rust-colored Shetland hat, a lavender shirt and soft tan chukker boots; the next morning he'd show up in a flamingo-red shirt with stripes, twill riding trousers and an Irish tweed cap. An addition to his costume was a unique boomerang-shaped scarf pin, fashioned from the shoulder bones of the tiger he'd killed in India. "They're lucky Bengal bones," he explained. "As long as I wear these nothing on the picture can go wrong." Then he laughed uproariously.

Final sequences for *The Roots of Heaven* were to be shot in the Forest of Fontainebleau on the outskirts of Paris. Huston's scouts had picked the spot—a sandy plateau, ringed by trees and boulders —in an effort to duplicate part of the African locale. (These would be "matching" scenes; when spliced into the film it would be impossible to tell that they were not obtained in Africa.)

Several dozen Negroes had been recruited from St. Germain des Pres for these matching scenes. They were supposed to dance wildly around a car containing Flynn and Greco, brandishing spears and howling fiercely.

At the first take Huston groaned in displeasure. "They're not looking hostile enough," he said to an assistant. "Go tell 'em I want lots more scowling and spear-shaking. God, you'd think they were out there as a welcoming committee."

While waiting for another take Huston moodily played *boules,* the French game in which small metal balls are tossed into the air. He was good at *boules,* as he was at most competitive pastimes, and was winning from the extras.

A shrill animal howling, followed by pistol shots, broke up the game. Directly up the hill, behind the massed trees, two hyenas (imported from a local circus) were locked in battle. One had bitten off the other's tail. The trainers were howling louder than the hyenas, firing their pistols and dancing about in helpless fury.

"Now, *that's* what those natives should look like," said Huston.

Flynn's death scene was the last to be shot, with Greco set to discover him as he lay dying. She is grabbed by the hunter who killed Flynn, struggles briefly, and is borne away by two natives.

Miss Greco threw herself into this final scene with surprising gusto. When it came time for her to struggle she kicked and scratched and knocked down the hunter. Then, still kicking, she was dragged into the brush.

"Fine, honey, fine," said Huston. "But, let's do it again."

Six takes were required to satisfy Huston, with the girl clawing and kicking her way madly through each of them.

"Blood disease be damned," said Flynn. "She's a tiger woman!"

"Well," grinned Huston, "Juliette *was* a bouncer, you know."

Greco nodded emphatically. "Heck yes," she said. "I knock a few heads together."

The Roots of Heaven was received by the press with disappointment; they had expected a much stronger vehicle than Huston gave them. The $4,300,000 film had few things in its favor: a solid performance by Howard, lush jungle footage, and some superb color work. Part of the blame could be laid on the murky script (written by the book's author, Romain Gary, assisted by Patrick Leigh-Fermor); the character of Morel had not been properly defined, and much of the dialogue was weak.

Time called it "an interesting but curiously unconvincing picture." *Films and Filming* commented on the director's approach to Morel: "In his attention to this character Huston indicates his continued respect and admiration for the individualist who goes his own way, using others only as practicable means toward his ends, and finding the ultimate reward in his own integrity."

Roots completed Huston's obligation to 20th Century-Fox; he had now signed with Hecht-Hill-Lancaster to make what he termed "a western Western." (Warner's had released *The Treasure of the Sierra Madre* as a "western"—for want of a better category—though Huston always claimed he'd never made one.)

The source for Huston's new film was a novel by Alan Le May, *The Unforgiven*, which centered on a controversial theme wherein the heroine (Audrey Hepburn) is revealed to be of Indian blood. She ends up marrying the white man she'd thought to be her brother (Burt Lancaster). The story is climaxed by an Indian attack in which the girl must fire upon her own people to save the man she loves.

The screenplay by Ben Maddow (who had worked with Huston on *Asphalt Jungle*) played upon this "modern" theme of racial prejudice against the setting of the Old West.

Audie Murphy was chosen for Lancaster's quick-tempered brother (re-uniting Huston and Murphy for the first time since M-G-M's Civil War) and silent screen great Lillian Gish was also prominent in the cast. Charles Bickford and John Saxon had substantial parts, as did Joseph Wisemen (portraying the mysterious Kelsey, who reveals that the girl is really a Kiowa).

"Believe it or not, this one wound up costing more than *Moby Dick!*" says a Huston aide who worked on *The Unforgiven*. "Hepburn and Lancaster got 300 grand each, to start with. The special sod house, where a lot of the action takes place, cost another 300 grand. Then there was John's salary as director—and he always gets star pay. Then Audrey fell off her horse down in Mexico and broke her back. This cut right into our shooting schedule. We flew all the color film to London for processing because John felt the quality would be better; then they'd air-mail it back to us each day. That wasn't cheap! Costs just kept piling up like mad—until the bill topped five million. Came close to five and a half before we finished. That's a lot of dough for playing Cowboys and Indians."

Most of *The Unforgiven* was shot in the rugged country beyond the old mining town of Durango in the badlands of central Mexico. On these raw, windswept plains, facing the foothills of the Sierra Madres, an authentic "soddy" was constructed. The house duplicated those built by Texas pioneers in the 1860s, but was far more complex.

Built with a steel frame, the structure was invisibly hinged to provide breakaway walls which could be rolled back to admit the camera crew. A man-made hill covered it and was layered with real grass and cactus.

"This sod house was the site of our big Kiowa attack," says Huston, "and—in its own way—was almost as ingenious as the whales built for *Moby Dick*. It served as a studio as well as our main set because we did our film cutting right there, in the back of the house under the artificial hill."

Lillian Gish became very fond of Huston during the production. "He's another D. W. Griffith," she told the press. "They're of the same mold."

While Hepburn's back was mending, following her accident, Huston decided to visit his adopted son, Pablo Albarran, who was now living in Cuernavaca. The boy was married and had a son of his own whom he had proudly christened John Walter Huston Albarran.

"Can you beat that Pablo!" exclaimed Huston. "Here he is a family man with a lovely wife and kid. And do you know what he does for a living? Shoots Mexican cheesecake! Imagine! Pin-ups for Mexican magazines! Boy, isn't that Pablo something?"

United Artists released *The Unforgiven*. Although it possessed Huston's usual excellent photography—with Franz Planer, who worked on *The Big Country*, behind the color camera—and was directed in a skilled, fast-paced manner, the film suffered from poor editing and an exceedingly unrealistic Indian attack.

As one reviewer pointed out: "A fully-armed war party of real Kiowas would have swept over that sod house in short order, killing everyone in it. But *these* Kiowas were working for Mr. Huston, so they all flopped off their horses and bit the dust exactly as called for by the script. Audie Murphy's one-man rescue had all the believability of a single marine winning the battle of Tarawa."

The best Huston touch in *The Unforgiven* was a frightening and visually imaginative manhunt staged during a fierce windstorm, in which the ghost figure of Kelsey continually appears and vanishes in the swirling sand.

Basically, despite its high budget, this was an interim film for John Huston. He was about to embark on a major creative effort; he was set to direct Arthur Miller's tragedy-haunted story of *The Misfits*.

Chapter 15

MANAGING THE MISFITS

Good fiction inevitably finds its base in meaningful truth. For Arthur Miller, *The Misfits* grew out of a chance meeting with three Nevada cowboys early in 1956. The playwright had rented a small shack at Pyramid Lake, some 50 miles northeast of Reno, taking up this Nevada residence in order to divorce his first wife. A friend introduced him to a trio of mustangers who were heading for the dry lakes to rope wild horses. "We sell 'em for dog meat," one of the men told Miller. "Wanta come 'long and see how it's done?" Sure, Miller said he'd like to come along.

En route, he learned the history of modern-day mustanging. Prior to the last war, the mountains were full of wild mustangs and there was a substantial market for them as children's ponies. But as the herds thinned, and children began to want motor bikes instead of ponies, the market changed. Now the horses were sold to be slaughtered—and catching the wary, four-legged beasts had become highly mechanized: one man would flush out the herd by plane, driving them onto a dry lake; then the other men would pursue them by truck, roping as many as possible. Their catch was worth six cents a pound, as dog meat.

Miller realized that these men who followed the mustang trail were throwbacks. They lived as the cowboys of the early West had lived, and although their trade had degenerated they were of the same hardy mountain-and-prairie breed. Society had not tamed them.

"They represented, to me, the last really free Americans," says Miller. "They were misfits in our modern jet age, as were the mustangs they still pursued, and this fascinated me. I had to tell their story."

Miller did just that, selling a short magazine version to *Esquire* where it appeared the following year. By then, Marilyn Monroe had become the second Mrs. Arthur Miller.

"When the story was printed I thought that would be the end of it," says the playwright, "and I never had any idea of doing this for the screen. Not until Marilyn entered Doctor's Hospital in New York some months later. Then I began to talk about the idea with a photographer, Sam Shaw, and with John Huston."

Discussing his involvement with the project, Huston says: "Arthur told me the story while we were visiting his wife. Every day, while Marilyn was there, we'd meet in the hospital waiting room and he'd develop a little more of the idea. Several months went by and Arthur finally sent along a script. I got it in Paris, where I was completing *Roots of Heaven*. It was a *hell* of a script—and I wired back my enthusiasm. That kicked things off."

In expanding his original short story for the screen, Miller added a new character, Roslyn, to balance his lead cowboy, Gay Langland. ("Marilyn had wanted me to write a play for her; instead I wrote my first screenplay with her in mind as Roslyn.")

For Langland, Miller wanted Clark Gable. The veteran actor was in Rome, finishing another picture, when he received a copy of the screenplay. Gable's reaction matched Huston's—and he happily agreed to make the new film. Eli Wallach and Montgomery Clift were signed as the other mustangers, Guido and Perce, with Thelma Ritter added in a central role, as the cynical divorcee, Isabelle.

Miller and his producer, Frank Taylor, decided that *The Misfits* had to be made in its natural Reno locale, using wild mustangs for the action sequences which climax the story. In December of 1959 Huston and Taylor flew to Nevada to select locations. They would use the Stix house (where Miller had first met the real cowboys), parts of downtown Reno, a dry lake in the area and—for the rodeo scenes—the little town of Dayton, where it would be necessary to build an elaborate rodeo grounds (chutes, corrals, grandstands) and to modernize the facade by adding new signs and false fronts to some of Dayton's older buildings.

After the locations were set, Miller accompanied Huston to Ireland for two weeks of further script work.

Marilyn's starring role in *Let's Make Love*, with French singer Yves Montand, caused a delay in production plans—but by mid-July, 1960, cast and crew were assembled in Reno for the opening scenes. (Huston had determined to shoot Miller's script in strict chronological sequence.)

Russell Metty, Huston's cameraman on *We Were Strangers*, was shooting *The Misfits* in black and white since the director felt that color would intrude on the harsh qualities of the story.

Reporter James Goode, who tagged along to write a detailed account of the filming, was amazed at the variety of individuals connected with picture-making. "By the time production began," Goode wrote, "there were over 200 people on location, including: four on the camera, five on sound, eight on lighting, five on props, three on set decoration, a painter, a greenman (fake shrubs, etc.), a doctor, a masseur, a dialogue director, a script girl and a script man, four secretaries, a production assistant, two assistant assistant directors, a personal maid for Miss Monroe, a make-up man for each of the principals, a body make-up girl, a hairdresser, a stand-in for each actor, doubles for the rougher scenes (including a double for Gable's double), a still photographer, a publicity assistant, a dramatic coach, an auditor, an assistant auditor, a transportation chief, 20 local drivers, three pilots, 10 cowboys, a rodeo clown, six policemen, three watchmen, two dogs and their trainer, five stockmen with horses and bulls, a wardrobe man and woman, a seamstress, an assistant film editor, a five-man catering service, a whistle blower, plus various baby sitters for the men who had brought their wives and children."

Half of Reno's Mapes Hotel was taken over by this vast assemblage—and Huston immediately headed for the Mapes Casino,
where he was to become a "regular" at the dice tables. After a
disastrous run of bad luck he was asked if losing shook his confidence. "Not at all," Huston said with a bland smile. "I've never
thrown the dice when I didn't expect to win. The one great lesson
you've got to learn in gambling is that money doesn't mean a goddam
thing."

Clark Gable had gone on a crash diet in order to shed 35 pounds
for his role. He arrived in his sports Mercedes, looking tanned and
very fit. "This is an offbeat story," he said, "and the character I'm
doing is offbeat. He's lived between wild horses and wild women
all his life. The boundaries of Langland's world are the mountains
and plains; he has a hunger for women, but no trust in 'em. Mustanging is a natural thing to him, what he's proud of. Then this girl,
Roslyn, comes along and tells him that he's a butcher, sacrificing
these wild, free horses for so much dog meat. He fights her, doesn't
want to believe what she says is true, but finally comes to accept it.
She never tames Langland, but she changes his direction."

Huston was having trouble with one of the extras, a local bum
who had been hired to spin around in drunken imitation of a dress-
maker's window dummy. The fellow seemed unable to execute the
spin to the director's satisfaction. "He looks like he's posing," said
Huston to an aide. "Go out and buy him some booze, then bring him
back for a re-take."

Upon his return, with $20 worth of whiskey neatly stowed away
in his system, the bum did an excellent job. He was still spinning
when the scene was over.

Marilyn Monroe's constant companion on *The Misfits* was her
personal drama coach, Paula Strasberg, who dressed entirely in black.
As James Goode observed: "She was attired ominously in a black
silk dress covered by a black silk wrapper crowned by a long gold
chain bearing a collection of sorcerous gold objects. Then she had on
black silk stockings, small black slippers and a black veil enclosing
her head. Small, black straw fans, continuously in motion, provided
a stir of air in the 100-degree Nevada heat. Huston contended that
Paula portrayed a religious figure that pre-dated the Cumaean sibyl
of Greek mythology, but no one had the nerve to ask her about this."

Monroe herself, in startling contrast, was all blonde and moon whiteness. Her glowing body was incredibly soft, according to masseur Ralph Roberts, who gave her a daily rubdown. "The skin layer right under the surface was moist and deep, like no other woman's," claimed Roberts. "In the dark, her skin could light up a room!"

Marilyn's wardrobe was not extensive in *The Misfits*, but what there was cost a tidy amount: a wisp of a bikini was billed at $300; three lace slips ran to $700 each. And in view of the hours she worked, her cost to the production was excessive. "I can't function before noon," she'd say wistfully. "So it's just no use my being on the set before then."

This greatly annoyed the other members of the cast, and drove Gable to the point of rage—but they had to conform or scrap the picture. Reluctantly, they conformed.

The Misfits marked a homecoming for John Huston. His last eight films had all been made abroad, in various parts of the world, and not since *Red Badge* in 1950 had he directed on American soil. Relaxing beside the set, he talked of *Misfits* and of personal independence.

"Anybody who holds out against the accepted norm is a misfit," said Huston. "Take Gay Langland. I personally admire that kind of guy. Guido is flexible; he'd end up loving animals if the girl wanted him to, just to get the girl. He doesn't have any real code to live by. Perce is very simple and easy-going, but he lacks the dedication to personal freedom possessed by a man such as Langland. He doesn't lead, he follows.

"The girl doesn't defeat Langland; she just adds a new dimension to him. They decide to raise a child together and teach it to be brave. That's the whole point. Not stupidly brave, because you've got to figure out the eventualities intelligently ahead of time. But when the moment comes for action, whatever it is, a man must have the courage to close his eyes and *do* it.

"Me, I've always been a misfit in this industry. They can't quite figure me out. I've made some mistakes, some whoppers. I'm not sure I wasn't a better director before the war—back in the days when I didn't run the whole show. But I hate the system—and I'm free of it so long as I can tell anyone to go to hell in a bucket! I'm free to make a damn fool of myself or to do something wonderful. The choice is mine and that's what counts."

Huston arranged to have Harrah's Club, Reno's famous round-the-clock gambling palace, closed down in order to use its interior for some scenes with Gable and Monroe. This was the first time in years the club had shut its doors to the public, and the loss was estimated at $50,000 a day. Luckily, Huston was able to complete his scenes in just a day and a half, permitting Harrah's to resume its profitable 24-hour schedule.

Russell Metty informed Huston that he was putting up the money for an oil-well drilling operation—and did John want in? Sure, Huston said he'd take a flyer, and contributed $40,000 to the deal, adding: "I've always wanted to be an oil baron!" (The director had won $7,500 in just six hours at the Casino dice tables, and was in an expansive mood.)

On August 5, Huston's 54th birthday, a lavish party was arranged at the Mapes. Guests from Hollywood, Paris, Dublin, Chicago, New York, London and San Francisco were flying in to share the celebration. Count Ledebur from Austria would be there; Burl Ives was due, with guitar, from Kansas City; Mort Sahl promised to entertain—and a tribe of Paiute Indians were also on the way.

"John Huston's birthday is usually an international social event rivaling the opening of the Vienna State Opera House," declared a member of the press. "You don't attend it—you *survive* it!"

As part of the festivities, Chief Thunderface made Huston an honorary member of his Paiute nation, dubbing the tall director Long Shadow. Huston raised a glass to the chief. "I'm proud to be in the tribe," he said with fervor, "and I intend to be one of the best damn Paiutes there is!"

Marilyn Monroe became very sentimental over Huston. "Nobody would ever have heard of me if it hadn't been for John. He's meant a great deal in my life. Working with him again, after all these years, is so good! He's an artist with a camera—and he sees like a painter. John watches for the reality of a scene, then leaves it alone. He waits till he needs something before he comes in—and I think that's just a lovely quality."

Each evening after the day's shooting Huston returned to the dice tables, playing intently with large stacks of $25 chips. When he lost, he smiled; when he won, he left behind a "few hundred for the boys"—and all the stickmen were his pals. But more often than not he lost, standing all night at the crap tables, endlessly wagering on each roll of the dice.

After two solid weeks of this, he told Miller: "God, Arthur, this is harder on my constitution than Africa *ever* was!"

As Guido, Wallach was supposed to pilot a plane—used by the mustangers to drive wild herds out of the mountains—and Huston found a 1939 Meyers two-winger which he rented for the bargain price of $20 per day. The weathered Meyers was actually flown by Ken Slater, a veteran stunt pilot who had begun his long career with *Dawn Patrol*. It took all of Slater's skill to handle the cranky, underpowered old plane, and on his first filmed takeoff he hit the tops of some fruit trees, but kept flying.

Wild mustangs were next on Huston's list, and he told the wranglers to go catch some. Bill Jones, head wrangler, commented on the fact that this was the first time that genuine wild horses had been used in a film. "We got 'em right here off the mountains," he said. "Got one mustang stallion that's a mean sonuvabitch. He stands gentle, then lets you have it with both feet. Fast as lightning, he is. He'll come right at you. Mr. Huston needed some Brahmas and some steers for the roping and bull-dogging scenes, and he wanted 'em rough. Well, we brought in the roughest there is in the U.S. and he looked real pleased. Fine man, that Mr. Huston. Really loves a good animal!"

On August 16, Huston calmly lost $15,000 at the Mapes, then headed for Dayton and the rodeo sequences.

One observer described Dayton as "a semi-ghost town sprawled in the sun south of Virginia City. Behind it rise the round-backed, red-clay mountains of the Comstock Lode. Nothing but sage brush grows here—and in mid-summer the thin, high, rarefied air boils up to 110 degrees!"

The character of Perce called for Clift to ride a bucking bronc in the Dayton rodeo, and Clift had been practicing for these scenes with professional circuit rider Dick Pascoe. At a rodeo at Pocatello, Idaho, Clift had been helping Pascoe mount a Brahma bull when the beast tossed up its head and slashed the actor across the bridge of his nose.

Clift was therefore understandably nervous about a chute scene in which he would mount a wild bronc. The horse was quite skittish, snorting defiance at the Hollywood star. With the camera's eye upon him, Clift settled professionally into the saddle—only to have the bronc rear back violently against the side of the wooden chute. Clift's shirt was nearly ripped from his back. Huston thought this made a fine shot.

The director had a much rougher time recording a sequence in which Pascoe (doubling for Clift) was to be thrown from a Brahma bull and rescued by Gable's double. The spotted black-and-white bull personally chosen by Huston refused to cooperate, leaping the corral fence in a dedicated effort to avoid his film debut.

"He saw some good-looking cows out there," said Huston. "So he figured to go after them like any red-blooded bull would figure to do. Personally, I admire his spirit!"

The extras (hired as spectators) did not find the Brahma's spirit so admirable, particularly when he landed square in their midst during one of his amorous jumps. On another flight, the bull sought refuge in Gold Canyon Creek. At each escape attempt, the wranglers would patiently ride out and fetch the stubborn animal back for another take, causing one of them to remark: "That dang critter's harder to get on the set than Monroe!"

Huston finally recorded the footage he was after—then cheerfully retired to the dice tables.

Reno's power lines were burned out during a fire in the area that same month, and the Mapes Hotel lost its electricity. (In the Sky Room stripper Lili St. Cyr was forced to perform her act by candlelight.) Huston was upset. He instructed the film crew to haul in its generator from Dayton and illuminate the Mapes Casino. Thus, the director's gambling was not affected.

Due to this sudden power failure, an elevator operator was trapped between floors. Huston felt that the fellow should be fed Scotch "to keep up his courage" until power was resumed. He therefore handed the operator drink after drink through a small aperture at the top of the elevator. When emergency power activated the cage, and the elevator doors opened in the lobby, the glaze-eyed operator pitched out flat on his face to the carpet. Huston looked down at him sadly. "Guess he just *isn't* a drinking man!"

On August 27, with location work three-quarters finished, Marilyn Monroe was flown to a Los Angeles hospital in a state of nervous exhaustion. Huston had ordered her to bed. Pressmen asked him if he wasn't worried about the picture. "To hell with the picture," he told them. "The girl's health is at stake. If Marilyn gets proper rest at this point she'll be okay again. The picture will just have to wait. Me, I'm going camel riding."

Huston had already announced his entry for the Labor Day Camel Race at Virginia City, and would be competing against his friend Billy Pearson. "Frankly, I'm looking forward to it," he said. "Never been on a camel, but I guess that's no handicap cuz neither has Billy. I'm riding for the Phoenix *Gazette* and Pearson is representing the San Francisco *Chronicle*. It's shaping into a battle of giants."

The gala day began with a champagne breakfast in Reno; then the contestants climbed into several antique autos for the drive to Virginia City.

"Huston's machine was a 1914 American Underslung," says columnist Herb Caen. "When the car failed on a hill Johnny shot it in the radiator and caught a bus."

The director's riding garb for the race was bizarre even by Huston standards. James Goode described the costume: "It began with a pair of English riding breeches—to which was added a mauve shirt with a Faubus-for-President button pinned to one pocket, a straw hat with a Madras band, a silk scarf and red tennis shoes. The total effect was memorable."

Huston's camel was a five-year-old two-humper named Old Heenan, which had never been ridden. ("Neither have I, so that makes us even!") Pearson's mount was a moth-eaten 50-year-old one-humper named Izzy.

"The older a camel is the faster he runs," Huston assured the disgruntled Pearson. "Take my word for it, Billy, as an expert in ancient camel lore."

The third entry, from Indio, was a 15-year-old female named Sheba, to be ridden by a brave local citizen.

As the three contestants were gingerly helped aboard their steeds, looking uncomfortable and apprehensive, the camels became enraged, seeking to bite the legs of their unwanted riders. Leather muzzles restrained them.

At the shot from the starter's pistol, Huston's dromedary bolted madly away from the line, forging ahead of the horsemen who were supposed to be leading the race. The luckless rider from Indio was instantly thrown to the ground—but Pearson stuck with Izzy who lived up to Huston's prediction and shot off at top camelpower. Unhappily for Billy, the angry beast galloped sideways into the crowd, jumped a tiny sports car, mashed in the trunk of a new Lincoln—then aimed its ugly neck for Piper's Opera House (where Lily Langtry used to sing) which was at the top of a steep hill one full block off the official course. Pearson let out a yelp, then ducked behind Izzy's hump as they clattered up the hill and through the doors of the opera house. Inside the lobby Pearson quickly parted company with his camel, shouting: "I concede! I concede!"

Huston was the undisputed winner, crossing the finish line without his hat, hair streaming out behind him, teeth bared in a wide smile of triumph.

"I owe my splendid victory to a deep understanding of the camel," he declared in a radio interview after the race. "You're really living when you're up there between those humps. It has its ups and downs, but so has life."

Asked how he had originally mounted Old Heenan, the director grinned. "Well," he said, "I asked a young lady if she'd give me a leg up before the start, but she looked rather shocked at the question so the job was given to someone else."

And what did he think of his chief competitor, Billy Pearson?

"He's an obvious disgrace to the camel-riding profession. He rode over parked cars, widows, orphans—in fact, there are camel-stunned babies scattered all over these historic hillsides. It is a scene of carnage, owing to Pearson's shocking mismanagement of his mount. He just doesn't belong up there on the hump of a camel."

Further along in the interview Huston claimed that a sniper had taken a shot at him just at the start. "It must have been Herb Caen," he said. "Herb lost his girl to me, and these *Chronicle* people are awfully poor losers!"

The announcer pointed out that the shot had been fired by the starter, but Huston chose to ignore this information. "It was a foul start," he said. "But then, when you really come down to it, anything to do with camels is foul. That's why I'm retiring from the sport."

By September 6, having flown back to Reno, Miss Monroe was ready to resume shooting. She was still taking far too many sleeping pills, and Huston said of her (at a much later date): "She was always sensitive, nervous and goaded." In Marilyn's wake came rumors of an impending separation from Arthur Miller, based on her romantic attachment to Yves Montand. Miller, who was working closely with Huston on the set each day revising and polishing every page of the script, refused to comment.

The production was $416,000 over budget when Huston's cast and crew headed for their dry lake location east of Dayton to film the wild mustang hunt. The location embraced 15 miles of dead-flat lake bed surrounded by mountains and thick with alkali dust. Gable drove out in his 300 SL, hitting 140 mph on one long straight. ("She'll do 160 with the right axle ratio!")

Clift and Gable were strapped into the back of a pickup truck and given ropes.

"Now, you boys pretend to lasso some horses," said Huston.

Once roped, another noose connected to a large truck tire was thrown over the neck of each mustang, functioning as an anchor. Doubles would be used for most of the actual roping, but Clift and Gable had to look professional in the close-ups. In one bit of action out on the lakebed, which could not be faked, Clift struggles to hold a fighting mare, slashing his hands on the rope; they were lacerated and bleeding by the end of this scene.

At 59, Gable found himself tiring more quickly than he had anticipated. He'd lost weight much too fast in his crash-diet for *Misfits,* and now this factor was contributing to his exhaustion. But the actor did not complain.

That weekend Huston was disappointed at having to miss a snail race in San Francisco. ("We were backing an entry named Miss Fit, but she lost and they ate her after the race.")

A resumption of Marilyn's illness caused another delay, and Huston went sailing while the actress rested. She was back on the set by September 20—for a bedroom scene in which a nude Monroe is awakened by a tender morning kiss from Gable.

"Miss Monroe wore a bedsheet," says a Huston aide. "But her

right breast was exposed in the seventh take, which John okayed. Much later, after a big argument, that take was cut from the final print."

Jim Palen, doubling for Gable, survived an extremely tricky scene in which he appeared to be attacked by a wild stallion. The horse took his part seriously, kicking Palen in the head. Doctors feared a fracture, but Palen's skull was intact. (After being kicked twice more, he began wearing a crash helmet under his Stetson.)

There was jubilation on the set when Gable revealed that he was to become a father in February. He passed out the news with a delighted grin, saying: "I guess there's still some life in the old boy yet!"

Huston was not so delighted with his recent gambling luck at the Mapes. He had just dropped another $5,500, bringing his total loss at dice up to $50,000—"Which is almost as much as I'm getting paid for the whole damn picture!" (Actually, Huston was being paid his usual $300,000.)

The script called for several close shots of Langland as he was dragged across the lake by the wild stallion. Huston utilized a truck on which the camera was mounted, aimed to shoot directly down at Gable as he was pulled over the dusty lake bed.

"How fast do you want me to pull him?" the driver asked Huston.

"At the speed of a galloping horse. About 35 miles an hour."

Protected by heavy leather chaps, Gable was dragged for 400 feet through the choking alkali before Huston got the footage he wanted.

"You okay, Clark?"

"Yeah," said Gable, scowling up at Huston. "With no thanks to you."

Other sequences called for the actor to be knocked down and dragged by the horse—and to run briskly behind Guido's departing truck. Yet these action bits seemed to have no ill effect on Gable, and he appeared in good health on October 18, the last day of location shooting.

By the first week in November, at Paramount's Stage 2 in Hollywood, Huston called Gable in to complete his final scenes. Langland cuts the stallion free and goes off with the girl to begin a new life with their child-to-be. "I think this is the best thing I've ever done," the actor told Huston on November 4. "Now all I want out of life is what Langland wants—to see that kid of mine born."

But Gable was not fated to witness the birth of his son. He suffered a heart attack the following day, and died on November 16, 1960.

"I can't quite make myself believe he's gone," said Huston. "Clark was going to star in the Kipling picture for me. We had plans for it . . .

"He was one of the few holdovers from the days of the champs, and his film career had the same sweep and color as Dempsey's ring career. You can put Gable's name on the list with the Babes, the Galloping Ghosts, the Flying Finns . . . They called him King out here, and he rated the title. His throne, I fear, will remain empty for some time."

Paralleling Gable's death came the official breakup of Miller's second marriage—which was the beginning of the end for Marilyn Monroe. With her tragic death in 1963, *The Misfits* became her last completed film.

Costing a final $4,000,000, this film earned the dubious distinction of being the most expensive picture ever made in black and white. Critical reaction was varied at its release early in 1961. Many reviews commented on the heavy-handed symbolism of Miller's script and on such lines (spoken by Guido) as: "I can't make a landing and I can't get up to God!"

Time loosed its full arsenal of adjectives, calling the film: ". . . terrible . . . clumsy . . . obtuse . . . disgusting . . . raucous . . . ponderous . . . wooly . . . glum . . . rambling . . . banal . . . and fatuously embarrassing."

The *New Yorker* spoke of Huston's "deft" direction, and called *The Misfits* "almost continuously absorbing"—but ended by deeming it "a dramatic failure of considerable dimensions."

For John Huston, *The Misfits* represented a major creative effort, and if the result failed to match the overall attempt he could not be faulted for trying.

The tragedy had ended—and other projects awaited the director's attention. *Freud* was one of them.

Chapter 16

FREUD AND ADRIAN MESSENGER

The career of Sigmund Freud had long been a source of fascination for John Huston, and when he was finally ready to film Freud's life, in 1961, the director made a statement regarding his aims: "We have chosen a five-year period, from 1885 to 1890, when Freud was at a critical stage, fighting to prove that his theories were valid . . . I would call this film a species of thriller—a mystery of a very special sort in which the assassin Freud sought lies hidden deep—within each of us. My primary aim is to shock audiences into a recognition of their own murky, psychic motivations."

Charles Kaufman (who did the final screenplay in collaboration with producer Wolfgang Reinhardt) had become intrigued with Freud's work while filming *Let There Be Light* with Huston after the war. In 1948 he had approached 20th Century-Fox regarding a screen adaptation, but Freud's daughter (Anna) warned them that she would not allow a film biography to be produced. Ten years later, in '58, Freud's eldest son (Ernest) vigorously protested another proposed cinema version.

"By then we were ready to ignore such threats," says Kaufman. "Freud belongs to the ages—and we found that his life could be dramatized without the permission of his heirs, providing we portrayed no living characters and did not malign the subject."

In January of 1961, directly after he had finished editing the final print on *The Misfits*, Huston discussed a script which had been written by Jean-Paul Sartre. "It ran to a thousand pages," he said, "and would have made a 10-hour film! Well, we tried to work with it; we cut the thing in half, then began paring it down page by page. But there were problems."

Eventually Huston discarded Sartre's script and settled on the Kaufman-Reinhardt version.

Montgomery Clift's work in *Misfits* had so pleased Huston that he chose this actor to star in *Freud*. Clift exchanged his cowboy hat for a beard in preparing for the part.

"Monty has a photographic memory," says Huston. "He's one of those rare people whose brain is a sensitized plate as far as visual impressions are concerned. Yet he works very hard at perfecting a part, sometimes sleeping only a couple of hours a night when he's doing a picture. We filmed most of this one in Munich, and he only went out on the town seven or eight times during the months of shooting there."

In all, Huston spent six months in Munich and Vienna on this film. He was amazed at the calm reaction of the Vienna citizens. "Many of them had never even *heard* of Sigmund Freud," says Huston.

Illness or injury appears to be a part of every Huston production, and *Freud* followed the pattern. Universal dropped an estimated $600,000 in lost time when Clift developed bilateral cataracts. This malady, combined with a growing anxiety state over his role in the picture, required hospitalization. In defending himself, the actor declared: "This was surely the hardest part I ever did. For one thing, they kept changing the script on me. I'd go to bed knowing one set of lines and wake up to another whole new scene!"

Huston appeared onscreen for a trailer dealing with *Freud*, and narrated the film itself.

Again, the critics were split over the merits of a John Huston picture. The *Saturday Review* stated: "Despite such virtues as Huston's own beautiful reading of his lofty prologue and epilogue . . . the picture seldom touches any human level." Bosley Crowther, of the New York *Times* called it "a daring . . . fascinating drama . . ." and cited the direction as "graphic." *Time* reversed its stand on Huston, saying: "This is a taut, intellectual thriller . . . directed with dominating intelligence!" *Daily Variety* was disenchanted: "Alas, not even the keen and fruitful imagination of John Huston can quite isolate the personal drama of the man from the dry, impersonal, somewhat stuffy and pretentious text . . . from which the dramatic seed never quite escapes."

England's *Films and Filming* found that *Freud* was "twenty years out of date, a period piece in every sense of the word . . . This looks and sounds exactly like a belated addition to the Warner waxworks of the late thirties . . . although there is one rather good, sustained passage in which Susannah York is twice taken through the details of her father's death until she is forced to admit that he died, not in a hospital, but in a brothel . . . The style seems to be less Huston than William Dieterle in his biographical period."

Placed in general release as *The Secret Passion* (to increase box-office appeal) the film did not do well financially. Nevertheless, Universal signed Huston to direct a screen version of Philip Macdonald's mystery novel, *The List of Adrian Messenger*.

"They had a lot of writers try adaptations on this one," says Huston, "but Tony Veiller finally scripted it. We got Kirk Douglas, who owned the book, to star—and George C. Scott played the detective—but I guess the real lure for moviegoers was the gimmick."

The gimmick on *Adrian Messenger* involved the skills of makeup man Bud Westmore. He designed a series of artificial faces for Douglas and for guest stars Frank Sinatra, Robert Mitchum, Tony Curtis and Burt Lancaster, and it was up to the viewer to try and guess their identity. (At the film's end, each star stripped off his "other face" for the benefit of the audience.)

The Westmore disguises were wholly effective. Scenes with Mitchum and Curtis were shot at the entrance to Scotland Yard in London, and no one recognized the famous stars. (Each make-up job required up to four hours to apply.)

The story was climaxed by a spirited fox hunt which Huston filmed in Ireland, near Dublin, in County Wicklow. The director used several of his titled Irish friends in this sequence, including Lord and Lady Hempill from Tulira Castle, Viscount Powerscourt, Sir George Brook and Lady Melissa Brook, Countess Mount Charles and the Marquess of Waterford. (Huston also played a one-line scene as a rider—and his son Tony made his screen debut in a bit role.)

"I'd always wanted to film one of our hunts," says Huston, "and I had a marvelous time doing it!"

This episode in *Messenger* took 12 days to shoot, at a daily cost of $30,000—making it the most expensive fox hunt since the sport was originated in the late 1700s.

The busy Westmore was called in to transform a Corgi (a breed of tail-less dog) into a fox for the close-up camera. He attached special plastic ears and a long fox tail, then sprayed the Corgi reddish-brown. The confused animal rolled wildly about, shedding tail and ears, then took off for the nearest hedge. Westmore managed to solve their problem by locating two English foxes, which he rented for $20.

Scott became quite friendly with Huston during the production and defended the director against one writer's charge of "unfairly using people."

"I don't know that John ever uses people in any kind of really destructive sense," Scott was quoted as saying. "I don't think that's proper to say. However lonely a man Huston may be—and all remarkably individualistic men are lonely—I think he can depend on himself. He does not have to depend on the use, or *misuse*, of other people."

The List of Adrian Messenger was generally rated as just what it was meant to be: a casual exercise in detection and disguise with a bizarre plotline (involving a list of murder victims given to a detective who finally unmasks the killer).

"After the intellectual rigors of *Freud*, John Huston must have enjoyed relaxing with this genial thriller," wrote critic Raymond Durgnat. "In its amiable way the least serious of all Huston's films, it retains a rather cerebral flavor . . . He is so charmed with the spirit and ceremonies of the gentlemanly tally-ho that in the final sequence

Huston comes within striking distance of doing for fox hunting what Hemingway did for the bullfight . . . His direction is firm, sharp and atmospheric in giving us the panoply of a hunt in full cry."

As *Messenger* was being completed, Otto Preminger was casting *The Cardinal,* his new film for Columbia (based on the best-selling novel by Henry Morton Robinson). Preminger was looking for a colorful character actor to take the part of Cardinal Glennon, the crusty Bishop of Boston. In the film it is Glennon who takes the young priest, Father Fermoyle, on as his secretary, paving the way for an appointment in Rome. Fermoyle would be played by Tom Tryon, with Romy Schneider, Carol Lynley, Raf Vallone and John Saxon in other key roles. But who would play Glennon?

"Why not get John Huston?" suggested Nat Rudich, Preminger's executive assistant. "God knows he's colorful enough!" Ingo Preminger also urged his brother to offer Huston the part. "Phone him," said Ingo.

Huston remembers that call. "Otto never gave me a chance to say no," he declares. "I warned him that I hadn't done any real acting for many years, but he insisted. So I told him all right, if he met my fee, I'd do it."

Huston's fee: a painting by de Stael, for his collection at St. Clerans.

In January of 1963 the deal was set—and Huston was robed and acting by March.

Veteran actor Burgess Meredith, as the ailing Father Halley, dies onscreen while Glennon administers the Last Rites. The actor paid Huston a humorous tribute. "My death was at least three minutes quicker than scheduled because Huston was staring down into my face," said Meredith. "John was so depressingly good it hastened my end."

Preminger allowed Huston to deliver one line which was perfectly in character. When asked in the film how he had been getting along, John replied: "Fine, fine—just giving everybody a bad time as usual!"

At the completion of the picture, Huston requested that his robes be sent to him in Ireland. "I want to put 'em on and walk through town," he said, "with all those wide-eyed Irishmen wondering who in hell the new cardinal is!"

When this film was released the critics universally praised Huston's acting. Typical of the comments were those from *Time* and *Commonweal.* "Huston is superb—playing with a rip-snorting vitality that all but steals the show," said the news magazine. And *Commonweal* echoed this: "The performance that steals the picture is given by John Huston . . . a real and inspiring portrayal."

When Huston was told that he had been nominated for an Academy Award as Best Supporting Actor, he was shocked. "That's nonsense. There was only one actor in the family, and that was Dad. I could never top him and I don't want to try."

But a close friend saw it differently. "Don't believe a word he says! He's tickled pink with this nomination. John's a 100% ham at heart, and he's been on stage every day of his life."

Functioning again as a director, Huston was then deep in two major projects: he was working with Dino De Laurentiis on *The Bible,* and with Tennessee Williams on *The Night of the Iguana.*

The tent was going up—and Huston's Circus was ready to roll. Its next destination: Puerto Vallarta, Mexico.

Chapter 17

MISERY AND MIRTH IN MISMALOYA

In assembling the outrageously variegated cast and crew for *The Night of the Iguana,* John Huston surpassed himself. The tangled webwork of marital inter-relationships which Huston fostered with *Iguana* was unique in cinema history, and will doubtless never quite be matched in the future.

There was Richard Burton, fresh from *Cleopatra* via Wales and Shakespeare, who was accompanied by Cleo herself, Liz Taylor, who was still wed to her late husband's pal, Eddie Fisher. (Eddie didn't show up in Mexico, nor did Mrs. Sybil Burton, which was one of many blessings.) Burton was the star of *Iguana;* Liz was there to make sure he didn't involve himself with his three female co-stars: Ava Gardner, Sue Lyon and Deborah Kerr. Ava, fresh from Madrid and bullfighters, along with her brother-in-law, her two maids, a secretary-accountant, and her Hollywood hair stylist, romped about with Tony, a local beach boy, in her $15,000 Ferrari. Now single, she had once been married to Artie Shaw, whose current bride was John Huston's last ex-wife, Evelyn Keyes. Miss Kerr's second husband, Peter Viertel, was not only Huston's out-of-favor ex-scripter, but had once been "very taken" with Miss Gardner in Europe. Sue Lyon, cinema's celebrated *Lolita*, entertained her boy friend (and fiance) Hampton Fancher III, whose current wife was sharing location quarters with Sue's mother. Then there was Skip Ward (playing Sue's love interest in *Iguana*) whose wife was miffed at him because his girl friend, Julie Payne, had come down to Mexico to say hello. Author Budd Schulberg was very much onscene, having once been the husband of Virginia Ray, who had married and divorced Viertel before he linked up with Deborah Kerr, after she left her first husband. Herb Caen was there with his wife—and Burton's agent, Hugh French, was accompanied by his assistant, Michael Wilding, who was one of Liz Taylor's numerous legal mates. Mike was there to publicize Burton who was thinking about marrying his (Wilding's) ex-wife. Then there was the play's author, Tennessee Williams, with Freddy, his quiet friend, and Gigi, a tiny dog prone to Mexican sunstroke. Tennessee had never married anybody.

Additionally, Liz had imported her own secretary, a British cook and chauffeur, a male secretary for Burton and three of her children (by two of her ex-husbands). In Mexico, she also hired an ex-boxer, Bobby LaSalle, for a bodyguard, Ping-Pong opponent and sparring partner for Burton. Sue was accompanied by her schoolteacher-companion, Eva Martine, a beauty of 28, who had once admittedly smoked opium for two months.

Huston's chief photographer, Gabriel Figueroa, was normally a quiet, sensitive man—but when he drank (and in Mexico everyone drinks) he turned into an opera singer of considerable lung power; shutting him up, once he began singing, was an all but impossible task.

Adding yet more color to this bizarre assemblage was the man they called El Indio, Emilio Fernandez, a gun-toting director whose violent nature often got the best of him. (He'd shot his last producer.) When Taylor and Burton first arrived in Mexico, Emilio rushed into the cabin of their plane, grabbed Liz by the arm and shouted: "Follow El Indio! You will be safe with me!" Fernandez was sporting his six-shooter—but this had not daunted an enraged

Burton. "Get this bloody maniac off the bloody plane before I bloody well kill him!" The crewmen quickly disarmed El Indio and led him away as Burton swore lustily at them in Welsh.

"Contingencies are bound to arise," admitted Huston after being informed of the encounter. "Emilio's only weakness is his tendency to shoot people he doesn't like. Luckily, he did not fire upon Richard. This means he likes him. I'm sure they'll adjust to one another."

In all, 130 members of the *Iguana* troupe would have to adjust to one another—not including the horde of reporters and photographers due to descend on the location site during the months of filming in Mexico.

"John's as happy as a kid at Christmas," said Ray Stark, who was producing *Iguana*. "He just loves the idea of making a picture with all these neurotic people. Right now he's out buying guns for me and the cast!"

Huston duly presented six gold-plated derringers to Stark, Burton, Sue, Liz, Ava and Kerr. Each gun came in a velvet-lined box, containing five golden bullets—which were engraved with the names of the other five recipients. (Wisely, Huston had seen to it that none of the bullets carried *his* name.)

The salary of each *Iguana* star reflected his or her box-office worth. Burton was getting $500,000; Gardner, $400,000; Kerr, $250,-000; Sue Lyon, $75,000. When a reporter asked Miss Lyon why she didn't demand more, based on her success as *Lolita*, she grumpily replied: "Remember, I'm *only* 17! The rest of these people are *ancient!* I'm not going to let Hollywood ruin me the way it's ruined Liz Taylor, Deborah Kerr and Ava Gardner!"

Sue's mother proudly told a reporter: "Sue's *so* intellectual! I don't know how she *got* so intellectual. None of my other children are that way."

The original locale of *The Night of the Iguana*, as written by Tennessee Williams, was Acapulco—but when someone suggested to John that he should film the story there he snorted in disgust. Huston wanted a location which would reflect the torment of his characters—and he chose Puerto Vallarta and Mismaloya, on the rocky, heat-plagued west coast of Mexico. Puerto Vallarta was a small village in which electricity was a new-found luxury, while Misma-

loya—recalled from a long-ago Huston vacation—provided the ultimate in primitive living; surrounded by a thick rain-forest, unmarked
on maps of Mexico, it could only be reached via dugout canoe, and
was a hotbed of insects and lizards. Prior to the arrival of Huston's
Circus, its only inhabitants were 100 Tarascan Indians.

Huston employed a crew of native laborers (headed by his art
director, Stephen Grimes) and put them to work building an exact
replica of a weathered Mexican hotel at the tip of Mismaloya, some
300 feet above the sea. This site, on a cove in the Bay of Banderas,
would serve for most of the filming—with earlier sequences in
Mexico City and Puerto Vallarta.

By late September, while 283 workers and 80 burros were slav-
ing away on the hotel, *The Night of the Iguana* got underway at
Puerto Vallarta. Liz had rented a four-story villa overlooking the
town—for a "bargain" price of $2,000 a month—yet Burton pre-
ferred to spend most of his off hours in local bars, swigging *raicilla*, a
paralyzingly potent blend of cactus brandy far stronger than tequila.
"If you drink it straight down," he was quoted as saying, "you can
feel it going into each individual intestine." To which Huston added:
"I think that's because they left the needles in."

Burton's role in *Iguana* was that of a drunken, end-of-his-rope
defrocked minister, T. Laurence Shannon, cast out by his church
and forced to earn a living by escorting elderly ladies on cross-
country tours. When one of the ladies finds Shannon with a young
girl (Miss Lyon) in his room she leads a campaign to get him fired.
They all end up at a sleazy out-of-season hotel run by Ava Gardner.
(Burton has sabotaged the engine of their bus in an effort to fore-
stall his unhappy fate.)

They are joined at the hotel by an impoverished sketch artist
(Deborah Kerr) and her father, described as "the world's oldest living
and practicing poet." (He's 96—as enacted by 75-year-old Cyril
Delavanti.) The drama is played out between these disparate characters, each motivated by personal hopes, fears, lusts. In the stage
version Shannon is ultimately destroyed; Huston and writer Anthony
Veiller decided to save him for Miss Gardner in the film—notwithstanding vigorous protests by Tennessee Williams. The bearded
playwright tried vainly to change John's mind, though he *was* pleased
with Huston's overall concept of his play.

This zany, hard-drinking group quickly attracted the wrath of *Siempre*, a Mexican publication which evidenced a marked distaste for America and Americans. "Our children of 10 and 15 are being introduced to sex, drinks, drugs, vice and carnal bestiality by the garbage of the United States: gangsters, nymphomaniacs, heroin-taking blondes . . ." *Siempre* called for the removal of the *Iguana* troupe, stating that "it is not too late. Responsible Mexicans can still save Puerto Vallarta . . ."

Despite this printed furor, Huston calmly continued to shoot his picture, declaring: "I have long since ceased to be disturbed by attacks from the press. And I am far too busy to spread any carnal bestiality."

Before setting out for Mismaloya, Huston prepared to film his busload of tourists as they are driven around some hairpin turns on the narrow mountain road above Vallarta.

Thelda Victor, a Huston aide who was also playing a bit part as one of the tourists, termed the scene "a near-disaster." She elaborated: "We were all in the bus, Burton and the rest of us, with Skip Ward driving. The sequence was being shot on the top of the highest cliff in the area—and going around one of the curves Skip got too close to the edge. The soft, dirt shoulder began to give way— and we all scrambled out, in a panic, as the bus teetered back and forth, half on the cliff and half off. After it was pulled back to solid ground, Burton walked over to the script girl, patted her behind lovingly and said: 'I just wanted to make sure we were still alive.' Me, I trembled for two days."

In addition to the hotel, which would serve as his main set, Huston had ordered 40 bungalows built as living quarters for cast and crew on the high Mismaloya peninsula. Burton wanted to pin down a vile rumor which had been circulated concerning a "dry" location. Sue Lyon said she didn't think that a bar would be built on Mismaloya; Deborah Kerr agreed with her.

"Preposterous!" Burton thundered. "Inconceivable! Whoever *heard* of a location site without a bar? In England, while working with Pete O'Toole in *Becket*, I was stoned for three entire days—and that was a much more religious role. I was the Archbishop of Canterbury! Why, a bar is absolutely *ethnic* to our culture."

Huston appeared, hand raised, to quell Burton's fears; he assured the actor that a bar had indeed been set up on Mismaloya.

The high, remote peninsula was extremely difficult to reach, even by water.

"There's no harbor at Vallarta," stated Stephen Birmingham, a visiting reporter. "You climb into a native dugout canoe on the beach—which they call the Beach of the Dead—then wait for a wave big enough to carry your canoe into deep water. Then you are paddled out to a waiting motor launch. There you stand up and leap for the other boat—which is always tricky since the rim of the launch is considerably higher than the rim of the canoe. Next comes the eight-mile trip across the bay to the peninsula itself. Disembarking at Mismaloya is equally nerve-wracking. You must leap from the launch onto a floating pier, where you wait till a wave carries the pier close to shore. Then you literally fling yourself onto some rusted iron steps leading to a kind of wharf, which puts you on dry land. Catching your breath, you doggedly tackle the 134 earthen steps which have been carved into the mountainside—to the pinnacle where Huston has his hotel. All in all, it's a trip to remember."

Liz insisted on her own launch, and ended up with a sizable yacht which lacked speed but was large enough to satisfy her. Miss Taylor's ex, Mike Wilding, had rented the craft as part of his duties as Burton's assistant agent. (He also thoughtfully provided picnic-basket lunches for the couple.) Ava Gardner wanted a craft to match the thrust of her Ferrari—and settled for a small speedboat, behind which she intended to water-ski the eight miles to the set each morning. Sue Lyon also got a private boat, as did Deborah Kerr, but both of these malfunctioned and were inferior to the Taylor-Gardner boats. A motor launch brought in food for the other non-boat members of the troupe.

Sue claimed she could not act without her regular supply of gefilte fish and red horseradish, so this was flown in daily from Cuernavaca. Liz demanded hamburgers with plenty of onions, and her desire was also met. Ava settled for Mexican beer.

Perhaps the most upsetting aspect of Mismaloya was its non-human population. As one bug-bitten victim reported: "The place was lousy with scorpions, midges, chiggers, civet cats, mites, mosquitoes, flies, fleas, beetles, mountain lions, snakes and giant land crabs. Turn on a light, and your wall is covered with insects. Walk outside, and a spider lands in your hair."

Liz made the mistake of wearing open-toed sandals, and got chiggers in her feet. These had to be dug out with a knife. ("They burrow under the skin until they find a vein. Then they enter your blood stream. After that, the only time you can see them is when they are passing across your eyeballs!")

Huston openly admired Miss Taylor's courage under the knife. "Boy," he said. "That Liz is sure a cool veteran of operations. She's had 30 of 'em to date. Someone is always putting the girl on an operating table and slicing her up. She's got lots of spunk."

Burton's remarks concerning Liz were not always as complimentary. "Look at her," he'd say as she approached him. "She walks like a French tart."

Liz appeared in a variety of bikinis as the shooting progressed—one of which she'd made from a discarded nightgown. It consisted of a pale pink band across her hips and a peek-a-boo bolero top. This outfit prompted Burton to remark: "Lordy! Now she *looks* like a French tart."

However, after a few shots of cactus brandy, Burton would forget all inhibitions and strip down to his shorts for a brisk swim. Miss Taylor would always attempt to shield him on these occasions.

"Quite obviously, Liz does not like anyone else to see Richard in his underdrawers," observed Thelda Victor.

Huston remained prudently silent on the subject.

When Sue Lyon was bitten by a scorpion the New York *Times* treated the incident as feature news—just one example of the impressive flow of press items emanating from Mismaloya.

"They're giving us ten million bucks worth of free publicity," declared Ray Stark. "We've got more reporters up here than iguanas."

El Indio was doing his part in keeping the press happy. He had erupted into violence at a tavern in Vallarta, causing a London paper to cable for details. The story, as they had it, was that Emilio had killed two gringo tourists with his six-shooter. Fernandez was quick to deny this charge. "I have not shot a tourist in seven years," he declared. "I merely knocked two of them unconscious after they had been rude to a shy señorita."

Sue Lyon was worried about her hair splitting. "Look, look, John!" she wailed. "The ends are all splitting! I've only been bleaching my hair three times a week. Will these split hair ends show in the picture?"

"No, honey," Huston told her. "They won't show."

"You swear it?"

"I do, honey. I swear they won't show."

Sue's over-affectionate boy friend, Hampton Fancher III, was a source of concern to several people, including actress Grayson Hall. She approached Huston after a scene, eyes blazing.

"I cannot act while those two lovers are necking in the corner," she said. "Here I am, trying to concentrate on my lines, with the two of them going at it hot and heavy on the sofa. It's just *damned* distracting."

Huston solemnly agreed. He'd been having his own troubles with young Fancher, who had very definite ideas on how *Iguana* should be directed. "The kid bugged Johnny," says a Huston technician. "Kept telling him how he should direct the scene. Can you feature the punk!"

When Burton added his own complaint to the scales Huston barred Fancher from the set. This sent Sue into a crying fit.

"If you wanta neck," Huston said, "that's okay. But just don't neck on the set, honey. It bothers the people who are *not* necking."

Ava Gardner also broke into tears—over her costume tests. Her attire for *Iguana* was definitely unflattering.

"Now, now, Ava," soothed Huston, "don't you worry about it. You're *supposed* to look a little beat-up in this one—so that's how we dressed you. But you'll be the hit of the picture. I promise."

"Do you swear it?"

"I do, honey. I swear you'll be the hit of the picture."

The busy director even had to use his charms on Deborah Kerr, whose usual good nature was finally ruffled during a sequence in which the set directions kept changing. "As I walk off, would you like me to balance a glass of water on my nose?" she flared.

Huston smiled gently. "By all means, Deborah—if you feel it will help the scene."

This broke the tension, and they laughed together.

The early warning which New York reporter Peter Evans had

received seemed most appropriate: "Just keep your head down, kid," a Huston aide had cautioned him. "They're handling dynamite in this playpen!"

Liz Taylor exhibited remarkable calm throughout the tense nights and days of the *Iguana*. She munched her imported hamburgers, switched bikinis, played with her three children (two by Wilding, one by Mike Todd), sun-bathed—and looked after Burton. Following one of his five-hour drinking bouts she confided to a reporter: "Richard *lives* each of his roles. In this film he's an alcoholic and an unshaven bum, so that explains his appearance and liquid intake."

Burton's liquid intake was awesome. His alcoholic moods alternated between bawdy hilarity and sullen gloom; only Liz seemed able to handle him on the latter occasions. Once, after several Mexican boilermakers, Burton fell out of a chair on the set, slashing his thigh. He waved away help and went on with the scene.

Liz was not satisfied with the manner in which Richard's official hairdresser arranged his locks, and kept fiddling with his hair, deaf to protests that it was fine the way it was. Burton finally let out a Welsh oath and poured an entire can of warm Mexican beer over his head. "*Now*, by God, how do I look?"

When Liz was desparately trying to make friends with Tennessee Williams' dog, Burton turned to the man beside him and said: "The woman is absolutely *mad* about animals. Takes a bloody menagerie with her no matter where we go. Here, for example. Over at the house in Vallarta she has a hare which sits in the bidet!"

Many of the reporters were disappointed that no one had been publicly seduced or divorced on location, although the Skip Wards and the Budd Schulbergs were often locked in verbal swordplay. (Later, after *Iguana* was completed, Sue and Fancher would marry *and* divorce in rapid succession.) Things livened up a bit when Ava lost her combustible temper and swore violently at the photographers, kicking one of them in the stomach.

She had become annoyed with rumors romantically linking her to Fernandez. "This is ridiculous," she stormed. "I have absolutely no interest in the man. None!" El Indio shrugged listlessly, saying nothing. (He seemed drained of vitality since Huston had ordered him to put away his six-gun for the duration of the film. "It's like asking Samson to get a crewcut!")

One of the braver reporters persisted in trying to confirm the romance rumor. "You *did* kiss Mr. Fernandez, didn't you, Miss Gardner?"

"Hell, yes," Ava said. "Everybody kisses everybody else in this crummy business all the time. It's the kissiest business in the world. You have to keep kissing people when you're penned up and working together the way we are. If people making a movie didn't keep kissing they'd be at each other's throats."

The next individual to get hit in the stomach was Burton. Liz had decided to test his muscle tone after he'd had a workout with Bobby LaSalle. "Richard's tummy is like a rock," she said admiringly, after solidly punching him three times. "I need a strong man, you know. We have some truly delicious fights. I just adore fighting with Richard."

Rain delayed production for two full days—and Huston passed this time playing endless games of gin rummy. During one of these, when a lady reporter asked him if the picture would be put behind schedule as a result of the weather, Huston grinned. "Hope not. We can't afford any overtime." He was reminded of *The Misfits*, when Clark Gable insisted that a clause be put in his contract providing for an overtime weekly paycheck of $48,000. Gable admitted that taxes would only leave him with $800 of this amount. "But Clark wanted the clause in there just to make sure we got the lead out of our butts," said Huston.

Miss Kerr, once again her tranquil self, was jotting down all that happened in a diary. In the midst of an entry one evening, she turned to Huston (who was absorbed in his gin hand) and said: "I can't help wondering what would happen if the rest of the world got wiped out by an atomic war—with us *Iguana* people as the only survivors. I suppose we'd have to re-populate the globe. The result would be interesting, wouldn't it?"

Huston murmured a slow yes-dear-it-would reply, intent on his cards.

Sue Lyon yawned. "I get so *tired* of being a glamorous star," she sniffed.

"Don't give us any of that crap, sweetie," put in Ava. "Not after the way you were hogging the camera in my scenes today."

"Now, now, dears . . ." murmured Huston.

Deborah sighed deeply and continued her diary.

Due to a new six-day work week, *Iguana* remained on schedule.

Huston's hotel set swarmed with visitors. The scene before the camera involved a brief exchange of dialogue between Burton and Gardner, in which he threatens to rip the phone from the wall. "In a pig's eye you will!" she tells him.

"Action," called Huston.

"I'm going to tear this phone from the wall," snapped Burton.

Ava came in right on cue. "In a pig's ass you will!"

"Cut," said Huston. Then he turned to Ava. "It is the *eye* of the pig we wish to concentrate upon. Can you remember that, dear?"

Gardner was not happy in Mexico. She moved five times during the course of the picture. And by the time Huston was ready to shoot one of her big scenes (in which she was to frolic in the midnight surf with two handsome beach boys) she was very nervous and edgy. Realizing the problem, Huston kicked off his shoes and waded into the surf with her, carrying two stiff drinks. After downing these, Ava brought off the scene without a hitch.

Liz was ever watchful when Burton and Gardner did a scene together, since he had admitted: "Ava gives me that old tingle!"

"I trust Richard completely," she said. "It's just that I don't trust Fate. After all, Fate threw us together in *Cleopatra*."

Dark-eyed, six-year-old Liza Todd, daughter of the late Mike Todd (Taylor husband #3) was having a mirthful time in Mismaloya. She boasted to another little girl: "Remember *Around the World in 80 Days?* My first daddy made that. My second made a movie, too, and my third daddy, Richard, makes movies all the time with my only mommy."

When Burton heard this he firmly corrected her: "Don't ever refer to me as your third daddy. I am *not* your daddy. Your daddy was Michael Todd, and he was a very wonderful man. Don't you ever forget that."

Huston would amuse Liza by lifting her high above his head, telling her that she was really a bird who had been magically turned into a little girl, and that she could fly away anytime she wished.

"John's a marvel with kids," said Ray Stark. "Kids and horses all adore him."

The Huston flair for unique costuming was advanced another step in Mexico when the director appeared in a billowing, floor-length muu-muu, cut from a wildly-striped Mexican fabric. One of the press women asked where she might obtain a similar garment for herself. Huston gave her a wink. "That's my secret," he said. "I'll tell you where to get one of these only if you promise faithfully not to wear anything underneath it."

Not to be outdone by Huston, Liz turned up sporting an eye-dazzling antique gold ring encrusted with rubies and pearls. "The King of Indonesia gave it to me," she informed the group. "Wasn't that nice of him?"

"I'm going to marry Liz for her jewels," cracked Burton. "And all that I offer in return is *myself*—which should be enough for any woman."

Liz took another punch at Burton's stomach as Huston ballooned quietly out of the room in his striped muu-muu.

Between scenes the following day Huston introduced his cast to Mr. Buckminster Fuller, an architect-engineer whose claim to world renown rested with the fact that he had designed several igloo-shaped plastic geodesic domes (called Dymaxian Houses), one of which was displayed at the Museum of Modern Art in New York. Mr. Fuller was in Mismaloya at Huston's invitation.

"The marvelous thing is," said Huston, "he can build these domes any size. Big enough to cover dozens of acres. I've been thinking of having him put up a giant one over Mismaloya. Lush tropical vines would cover the roof, creating a beautiful soft-green light for the interior . . . We could all live under this immense dome, sleeping as the Japanese sleep, on slabs of polished wood!"

More realistically, Huston had invested an undisclosed sum of money in Puerto Vallarta as a budding tourist resort. Mr. Fuller apparently represented an exotic afterthought.

Unexpected trouble was encountered in preparing the climactic scene in which a captured iguana is cut free by Burton (in the same manner Gable freed the stallion in *The Misfits,* providing a symbolic key to the film). Mexican iguanas are sluggish by nature and don't mind being tied up. This particular iguana was happy to be where

he was and did not fancy scampering off into the wet jungle. The
scaly fellow ignored broom handles—and an application of turpen-
tine on his tail only made him twitch slightly.

"I think he's a fan of mine," said Burton.

Huston ordered a technician to rig a charged wire, delivering
110 volts of electricity. "Prod him with that when I give the word,"
said the director. "He'll jump."

Huston gave the word, but it was Burton who jumped. It seems
he'd been touching the pebble-skinned lizard at that moment, and
the current passed directly into his hand, causing him to leap straight
up with an agonized yelp of pain.

A far less humorous incident occurred shortly thereafter when
an outer balcony on one of the cottages suddenly collapsed, hurling
two of Huston's men down the cliffside. One of them, Tom Shaw,
was badly injured—and was flown to a Los Angeles hospital.

"Here we go again," said another Huston aide. "On John's
pictures somebody is always being flown to a hospital. I'd say Shaw
was lucky to get off Mismaloya. It's like having a war wound; they
take you out of the battle zone and send you home."

Huston was so upset over the accident that he walked into
Thelda Victor's cottage and—with a single, Rumpelstiltskian kick—
knocked over the balustrade. "These damn natives make everything
out of sand," he declared. At which a set worker rushed up to inform
them that the roof of Cyril Delavanti's house had just caved in.

"God alive!" exclaimed Huston. "We'd better get this damn
picture finished before we're *all* covered with rubble."

By the end of November, well ahead of schedule, Huston had
completed *The Night of the Iguana* (though retakes subsequently
required another week). He threw a vast, end-of-picture party for
cast, crew, the press and assorted "cats, dogs and iguanas." The bash
was held at the restaurant-bar in Mismaloya, beginning at four in the
afternoon. It was a catered affair (all the way from California), and
the quality of the food was matched only by the quantity of the
liquor. A 15-piece mariachi band rapped out frantic Mexican folk
tunes, and tequila was amply provided by 200 local natives. By
evening, Huston's party was in full swing.

Thelda Victor describes part of the unrehearsed entertainment:
"A 20-year-old German girl, whose function on the picture was never

fully explained to me, executed a very sensual solo dance and wound up on the floor writhing like a snake . . . Ava Gardner looked suitably sexy in a harem outfit which Ray Stark had given her. The party lasted for 12 hours, and even John's pet iguana looked stoned."

Back in Los Angeles at the Beverly Hills Hotel, after his two-and-a-half-month stint in Mexico, Huston assured local reporters that filming *Iguana* had been "a most serene experience." (During much of the press conference he was absorbed in the study of a 200-year-old mastodon tusk uncovered on the trip.)

One of the pressmen questioned Huston's statement. "What about all the trouble you had? That guy with multiple fractures who fell down the mountain on his head . . . Miss Taylor's chiggers . . . Mr. Burton's thigh injury . . . all those cases of dysentery and food poisoning . . . Miss Lyon's scorpion bite . . . your wardrobe designer's broken toe—and what about Mr. Williams' dog? Didn't the mutt come down with sunstroke?"

"The misfortunes you enumerate are entirely accurate," admitted Huston, "but I try to overlook such things. One hopes for a good picture as ultimate compensation. In this instance, I think we have just that. After all these years I can smell a failure. And this picture smells fine to me!"

Most of the reviewers agreed; a sweet scent of success permeated *The Night of the Iguana.*

A critical sampling:

"Huston has put together a picture that excites the senses, persuades the mind and even . . . speaks to the spirit." *Time.*

"An absorbing film of rare content . . . distinguished by its cast and by Huston's directorial vitality." New York *Herald Tribune.*

"*The Night of the Iguana* is that fine rarity, an improvement on the play. Everything good has been retained and refined. Huston understands the heat and the rain forest and the sea as a kind of moral crucible." *Newsweek.*

"It reaffirms Huston's great skill . . . he has always had an innate gift for regulating, impassively but surely, the flow of his material; and here again he is able to set up and watch tensions within a tight group, letting the film seem to work itself out, as he did in such fine pictures as *The Maltese Falcon, Key Largo* and others . . . The dialogue is polished to a glitter and the story absorbs

. . . It seems that, of late, Huston has been merely resting his grasp and can triumphantly bring it to bear on really appropriate material." *Films and Filming.*

Iguana's scent was just as sweet at the box-office, and it quickly became one of the top grossers of 1964, topping $4,000,000. "It'll climb to at least four and a half in the U.S. and Canada alone," happily predicts Ray Stark. "Then there's John's big overseas following. We'll pick up another six million in Europe. They just love John in Europe! This one's a real blockbuster."

Based on the success of *Iguana,* Dino De Laurentiis looked forward with confidence to Huston's first all-out spectacle (to be made under his producership): the long-planned, high-budgeted version of the world's strongest best-seller, *The Bible.*

Was Huston worried about such a massive project? Of course not.

"It should be fun," he said. "I've always wanted to create the heavens and the earth."

Chapter 18

THE BIBLE—AND BEYOND

In June of 1961, when Dino De Laurentiis first announced that he intended filming *The Bible*, the cinema world was astonished at the magnitude of his plans. The picture, he said, would cost $40,-000,000 to produce and would have not less than *four* directors. It would occupy 11 hours of screen time. "This will be the greatest project ever attempted in motion picture history," he declared.

Over subsequent months Dino extended his plans. He now talked of *two* films, each to run for six hours, costing a total of $90,000,000! (*Cleopatra*, at a trifling $37,000,000, would be reduced to the status of a "cheapie".)

By 1963—as Huston was prepping *The Night of the Iguana*—Dino told the press: "This will cancel out all other films ever done on the Bible. Orson Welles will direct the Abraham and Isaac scenes; Robert Bresson will direct the Creation; Federico Fellini will direct the Deluge; Luchino Visconti will direct the section on Joseph

and His Brethren—and John Huston will have the responsibility of
giving the entire project cohesion and continuity. Maria Callas will
be Sarah, Mother of the Jews, and Sir Laurence Olivier will be God.
Stravinsky himself will write the music. It will be fantastic!"

Nobody disagreed with Dino. ("Sometimes he cries when you
disagree with him," says a Dinoite.)

In publicly announcing his film, De Laurentiis rented a huge
(270 by 60 feet) sign on Broadway, extending for an entire city
block between 45th and 46th, and had it painted to his specifications.
The sign's rental price was $100,000 a year, but, as Dino says, "I took
it for two—and got a rate."

By September of '63, however, De Laurentiis was forced to
admit that "there's been a little trouble." Welles tried to re-write the
Good Book; Visconti openly admitted he was only in it for the
money; Bresson didn't like Christopher Fry's script—and Fellini felt
he was "wrong" for the job. Sir Laurence was too busy to play God
and Miss Callas had her opera commitments. Also, nobody seemed
to want to give Dino 90 million, or 50 million, or even 20 million.
"We're doing it for much less," he said. "I now have the backing of
several Swiss banks, and I've assured them that the film can be made
on a sane, sensible budget."

Set at a modest $15,000,000, The Bible would run only three to
four hours in its final version, with John Huston as solo director.

Huston replaced Olivier and Callas with Peter O'Toole and
Ava Gardner. Stravinsky would still write the score—and there
would be a total of 77 sets, the majority of them to be built at Dino's
new studio on the Via Pontina in the plains south of Rome. An
unknown couple would play Adam and Eve.

"They must be innocence personified," said De Laurentiis. "For
Eve, we will find an actress who can be utterly natural without
clothes. Acting in the nude can be upsetting, and Eve must not look
upset."

Film scouts began a tub-thumping hunt for "a fresh-faced Eve."
Thousands of photos were submitted and rejected; 300 girls were
interviewed, among them pretty Nicoletta Machiavelli, a direct
descendant of the notorious Renaissance statesman. (Nicoletta's
father said no when asked if his daughter could be tested in the

nude.) A Texas minister offered his wife, insisting that she was
"blonde, shy and decently innocent."

While this big talent hunt ranged over the globe, Huston made
his own headlines, in January of 1964, becoming a citizen of Ireland.
In the Dublin office of Justice Charles Haughey, where Huston
signed the official documents, he stated: "I've lived in Ireland for
quite some while, and my children have grown up here. The step
I'm taking represents a sincere desire to get back to the roots of my
ancestors. I've had this in mind for a couple of years."

In March of '64, at the Writers Guild annual awards dinner,
Huston was presented with the Laurel Award "for a long and distinguished record of contributions to the literature of the motion
picture." John was delighted with the honor, and toasted his fellow-
writers with vintage champagne.

Just a month later, in late April, he turned up—with actress
Stella Stevens on his arm—for the Academy Award presentations.
His *Cardinal* nomination for Best Supporting Actor was a popular
one, and many friends in the industry were rooting for him to win.
("If Huston takes home an Oscar tonight," wrote *Times* critic Philip
Scheuer, "put it down as a private Hollywood joke: 'Well, at least
he can *act!*'")

The director and his escort were interviewed for television, Miss
Stevens wearing a low-cut dress which elicited enthusiastic crowd
response. "I just think it's all too wonderful that John is up for an
Oscar," she bubbled. "I just *know* he'll win!"

He didn't. Veteran Melvyn Douglas took the award for his performance in *Hud.* Leaving the auditorium, Huston was stopped by
a reporter who requested a statement. John grinned. "Ain't it a hard
road we travel—and Purgatory at the end!"

By May, having selected most of his final cast, Huston was
ready to begin the long months of location work for *The Bible.* Eve
was 19-year-old Ulla Bergryd, the willow-thin daughter of a Swedish
language professor. When Dino signed her, the girl was in her third
year at the University of Göteborg, majoring in social anthropology.

"Ulla speaks four languages," says Huston. "She's as genuine as
a fingerprint. One of Dino's boys found her in the Göteborg Museum
of Art. We tested her without clothes—and she looked innocent and

provocative, which is just what we wanted. In the Garden, you know, neither of these kids is supposed to know what sex is all about. They don't even know how to *kiss*."

Ulla was shaken by her first screen test. "All I could think about was that I didn't have any clothes on," she admits. "But Mr. Huston was so gentle and sweet with me that I guess I managed to do all right. At least I was hired!"

Michael Parks, a 26-year-old Californian, was selected for Adam after Huston had watched some footage of the actor. Parks, a rebel in the Brando-Dean mold, had bummed his way around the country —driving trucks, acting in coffee houses, working as a fruit picker. "I had a pretty fair job upholstering coffins," he says, "but I dig acting more." The footage Huston had seen was from *Fargo*, a then-unreleased film.

"The boy has a built-in kind of intensity," claims Huston. "He'll come across strong on the screen."

The other name stars in *The Bible* (in addition to O'Toole and Gardner): George C. Scott as Abraham; Stephen Boyd as Nimrod; Richard Harris as Cain and Eleonora Rossi Drago as Lot's wife (who turns to salt at Huston's command). Zoe Sallis, a sultry young Anglo-Iranian miss, was signed as Hagar, handmaiden to Sarah. (In Mexico, Zoe had played handmaiden to Huston.)

Noted photographer Ernest Haas was contacted for the Creation. "We sent Ernie around the world," says Huston, "in order to capture the essence of life itself. He's photographing the melting of snow, the beginning of a river, an erupting volcano, the trembling wings of a butterfly, the arrival of spring, the movement of the tides, the eye of a hurricane, sunrise and sunset, underwater plants. . . . All these will be edited into a graphic seven-minute montage sequence, using Stravinsky's special score, and poetically illustrating the theory that Creation is a never-ending universal process."

Locations in Sicily, Egypt and Italy would range from the slopes of Mount Vesuvius to the deserts of North Africa. Dino's studio in Rome would be the hub, where the more spectacular sequences (Tower of Babel, the Ark and the Deluge) could be properly controlled.

When newsmen asked the producer for the plot summery of his picture he told them he didn't have one, to go read the Book of

Genesis, chapters 1–22. "That's what we're filming," he said. "From the Creation through Joseph and His Brethren. We start in the Garden of Eden, go to Cain and Abel, then to the story of Abraham and Isaac. We'll have Sodom and Gomorrah, the Tower of Babel, Noah and his great Ark, the Flood . . ."

"Who's playing Noah?"

"We haven't decided yet," said Dino. "We're also undecided about the snake. We wanted Nureyev, the ballet dancer, but we couldn't lock up the deal. John got a nice 13-foot python to take his place. Weighs 102 pounds."

The reptile proved to be unsuitable. It stonily ignored Huston, looked bored, failed to slither properly and would not hiss on cue. As a setman remarked: "It was really something, seeing John trying to charm that snake. We finally had to sack him for one that really wanted to *act*."

The Garden of Eden was actually a palatial 180-acre lush seaside estate 25 miles north of Rome, which belonged to Prince Odescalchi. Huston had plastic flowers strewn about and painted the trees gold. A thin coating of vaseline was spread over the camera lens to soften the atmosphere. Special filters were also used to lend "a shimmering effect."

"First we were going to use single fig leaves on Adam and Eve," says Huston, "but we found we needed more than one each. So we had wardrobe whip up some fig-leaf girdles, but they looked like G-strings—so we just shot Mike and Ulla from unshocking angles. We naturally couldn't have outright nudity—and we also wanted to avoid any 'coy' behind-the-bushes stuff. What we have is in good taste."

Huston wasn't sure that Eve should munch on an apple. "No church authority—and we consulted with all of 'em—really claims that Eve bit into an apple. They all agree that it's a piece of Forbidden Fruit, but that's as far as they'll go. We just don't specify what kind of fruit."

Christopher Fry (who did *Ben Hur*) had sweated for two years on his script of *The Bible*. When Huston had first seen the result he'd been quite pleased.

"Chris was pretty miffed about what Dino did to his last script, for *Barabbas,*" John says. "This time he got a promise that his dialogue would be treated with respect."

When the sensation-bent Italian press heard about Dino's nude Adam and Eve sequences they dispatched squads of beady-eyed *paparazzi* to lens Ulla and Mike in the altogether. Huston was shooting on a closed set, but this didn't stop the dedicated *paparazzi*. They bribed set workers, crawled over palace walls, hung from trees and crouched behind bushes, snapping away at the undraped couple. And this despite the efforts of two dozen tough *carabinieri* hired to keep away these unwanted visitors. "Those rat-bastard photogs would fight to snap a shot of their own dying mothers," declared a member of the cast.

Ulla ignored the popping flashbulbs. She was attempting to adapt herself to all the trained lions, zebras, giraffes, cheetahs and assorted beasts. A baby leopard scratched Ulla's thigh when she tried to pet it, causing a problem.

"We shot her from the other side," says Huston, "where the band-aid wouldn't show. We had a similar snag with Parks. Had to shoot around his vaccination marks. Also, Ulla's long blonde wig— where it was pasted to her bosom—kept coming unstuck in the wind. But, all in all, we did okay."

Peter O'Toole reported a TV session with an interviewer who asked him how he prepared himself to play God. "Such an idiotic question deserved an idiotic answer," says Peter. "So I told him that I took cold baths, gave up drink and tobacco and submitted to a series of daily birchings to achieve a spirit of personal humility. And the bloody nit *believed* me!"

Huston was approaching his first big spectacle with a degree of caution, assuring the curious that he was not trying "to do a DeMille." He declared that while he was not a religious man he nevertheless had great respect for the Book of Genesis as "noble story telling."

The Tower of Babel and the Great Ark presented special problems. Genesis describes the Tower as "reaching unto the heavens," but a literal translation of this would have panicked Dino's Swiss bankers, so it was built in sections to give the illusion of great height. "The top was shot in Egypt and the bottom in Rome," says one of Huston's many associates. "We had a rough time in Egypt.

The scene called for 4,000 Babylonians and only 1,500 guys showed. John sent us all out in cabs to scour Cairo and grab anything on two legs. If a guy could walk, we grabbed him."

The Roman version of the Tower had 3,500 extras, heads shaved and backs loaded with baskets of plastic bricks, climbing the "outside staircases." Before the start of each scene a make-up man would trot around each extra, spraying him from head to toe with a solution called Clean Fly (designed to change pale-skinned Italians into nut-brown Babylonians).

Gardner and Scott toiled on the slopes of Mount Etna, where a plastic Sodom had been re-created; Cain slew Abel with the jawbone of a rubber ass; Lot's wife turned into a pillar of salt, via Special Effects; and Katherine Dunham's dance troupe was summoned "to provide the sin."

Huston was queried as to just how much actual sin he was willing to show. "There will be no visible obscenity," he said, "but you will know unspeakable things are going on."

A desert raid, led by Abraham against a robber tribe, and involving 45 camels, was delayed when one of the humped beasts refused to gallop fast enough to suit Huston. The director quickly put his Virginia City camel lore to good use—and managed to sweet-talk the scruffy animal into adopting a brisker pace.

The animals in Noah's Ark, however, were another matter. Over 300 had been brought down over the Alps (from Althoff's European Circus) and housed in a special zoo adjoining the studio. "We just wanted two of each—to go up the gangplank side by side —but they kept getting pregnant," says Huston. "And the noise . . . oh, God, kid—the *noise!*"

The two honey bears would get into a family quarrel which would upset the elephants and stampede the zebras. This caused the Siberian tigers to growl, the yaks to grunt and the sheep to bleat. The African lions joined in the chorus with thunderous roars, causing the Watusi bulls to bellow. The din was indeed formidable.

Italy's big news: Huston was growing a long, white beard. Which could only mean he was going to play Noah.

"Is it true?" an excited newswoman asked him.

"Yes, I shall be essaying the part of Noah," he admitted.

"How thrilling! Then you're the character with 700 wives!"

Huston smiled gently. "You must be thinking of Solomon, dear. I've only had four."

Dino was rushing hither and yon raising more money to finance the film. Five models of the Ark had to be constructed, the largest of them costing $300,000. It was 200 feet long and 60 feet high, made of hand-cut logs with a wide gangplank to accommodate its many passengers. Huston, in full beard and tunic, herded his trumpeting, howling, barking beasts into the Ark with the same calm patience he'd used in herding his actors up the steps to Mismaloya. It was all in a day's work.

"We've got everything in this one," enthuses Dino. "The first sin, the first skyscraper, the first love story, the first murder, the first flood, the first passenger boat. And with Ava Gardner as the Mother of the Jews! How can we miss making a fortune?"

Dino has the figures to back up his enthusiasm. The Good Book is worth stacks of box-office coin. Three of the top 10 all-time big-money grossers are Biblical films: *Ben Hur,* which took in $38,000,000; *The Ten Commandments,* which racked up over $34,000,000; *The Robe,* which grossed $17,500,000.

"And those figures are just U.S.-Canada," says Dino. "My picture will be re-showing 20 years from now. What's 15 million for a thing like this? It's a drop in the bucket!"

Huston admits he doesn't know how it will all turn out ("The step from the sublime to the ridiculous is a short one!") but he isn't too concerned. Many other cinema irons are in the fire: he looks forward to doing another Tennessee Williams vehicle, *This Property is Condemned,* in the South; he wants to film Brian Moore's *The Lonely Passion of Judith Hearne* in Ireland; then, of course, there's *The Man Who Would Be King.*

"I want Burton and O'Toole for *King,*" he says. "Been waiting a hell of a long time to do this one, and now it's shaping up at last. After that, who knows? Maybe *Montezuma.* All about the conquest of Mexico by Cortez and the passing of a superior culture. This would cost so many millions to make it would probably finish my credit! Then there's *Lysistrata.* I'd like to collect all the delectable female flesh in Christendom for this, put them into one big pot and stir well!"

Nearing 60, Huston has aged gracefully. He can still summon

tremendous energy and enthusiasm for a project, and the old fire still brightens his eye when he speaks of untapped locations and un-lived adventures.

"The Hindu-Kush—now, there's a place, kid," he'll tell you. "That's where I want to make the Kipling story. It's Afghanistan *and* Pakistan. There's one little spot, high up, where you can see things clear . . . A plane can land after the snow melts. Nothing's changed up there since the 1800s. God, what a spot for Kipling!"

For John Huston, each film is what he terms "a little lifetime." He says: "We are all within this small planetary system, the actors, the set workers, the technicians. We're all very close to one another. Then, one day, suddenly, it's over—and a whole life is over with it. You can never go back to it. . . ."

He talks about star quality: "The camera sees deep. Up on that screen a man can become a special kind of god. Bogie was like that, always bigger than life."

He talks of the friends, co-workers, associates who are no longer with him—Agee, Bogart, Gable, Monroe, Flynn, Capa, Heming-way: "Nothing can really hurt you much after you see your friends start to die. But, what the hell, I've still got a lot of living to do. I want to earn enough money to get a few Goyas, some Piero della Francescas, a Rembrandt or two. They never go sour on you. I've got a Greek head, the head of a horse, that was sculpted by Phidias for the Parthenon in 300 B.C. The horse is *there,* a thoroughbred. You can feel it, sense it, all that beauty and strength right there in the stone . . ."

John Marcellus Huston remains an enigma, a mystery, a man of quicksilver moods and high passions, the end product of all that he has ever done or been—boxer, reporter, actor, horseman, editor, artist, singer, writer, director, producer, practical joker, soldier, rancher, hunter, fisherman, collector, gambler, sailor, drinker, globe-trotter, Irish landowner, lover, husband and father.

He is the man who once made his secretary's dentist cry (on a bet that he couldn't), who wrecked a friend's plush dining room playing touch football, whose life was spared because the gun of an angry husband misfired when the nettled gentleman placed it against Huston's chest and pulled the trigger; he is the man who hid a famous actor's pivot tooth in a bowl of soup, who keeps the key to his liquor cabinet under one of his Academy Oscars, who—hating sentimentality—if often sentimental, a man who is pretentious, vain, practical, spoiled, precise, charming and irresponsible—who loves and despises his craft, who can't sit still unless he's lit a fuse somewhere, who ignores the boundaries and gleefully breaks the rules— a shocking spoiler with mad ideas and the catlike ability to land standing up nine times out of nine. Wild, dangerous, loving and lovable, hateful and hated, a rogue genius and an ageless rebel—he is all of these things. John Huston walks—in his long-legged, loose-hipped stride—into country where angels *and* devils fear to tread, and he's covered a lot of ground.

It's an odds-on bet he'll cover a lot more.

As Sydney Greenstreet said to Humphrey Bogart in *The Maltese Falcon:* "By gad, sir—I don't know what you'll say or do next, but whatever it is, it's bound to be extraordinary!"

THE PROJECTS OF JOHN HUSTON

Films and Plays: 1931–1965

Note: The following list of official writer/director/producer/actor stage and screen credits includes only those which Huston has completed as a professional—bypassing such early (acting) efforts as his work in *Ruint* (1925) and *Triumph of the Egg* (1925) and in the Chicago WPA production of *Abe Lincoln in Illinois* (1933). His book credits are listed in the Huston Bibliography, but no attempt has been made to index his magazine and newspaper writing. (It is worth noting that Huston's work has been published in *Esquire, Sports Illustrated, Theatre Arts,* the New York *Times* and the *American Mercury*). His close involvement in such films as *The Killers* (1946), *Quo Vadis* (1949) and *A Farewell to Arms* (1956) are fully discussed in the text, along with his partial involvement in *Background to Danger* and an untitled wartime documentary. It is impossible to list all of the projects to which he has devoted his time and enthusiasm over the years (although the text covers several of these). In the final chapter Huston's plans are discussed regarding *The Man Who*

Would Be King, This Property is Condemned, The Lonely Passion of Judith Hearne, Montezuma and *Lysistrata*. Earlier items under consideration were: an around-the-world documentary, an original sequel to *The Maltese Falcon*, stage versions of *The Iceman Cometh* and *Alouette* and films of *Jennie Gerhardt, The Idiot, The Blue Hotel, The Sleeping Prince, Matador, Typee, The Martian Chronicles, Macbeth, Ulysses, The Lark,* as well as an untitled Irish picture with Burl Ives and the life story of Robert Capa. Huston also talked of directing TV versions of *Lysistrata* and *The Devil and Daniel Webster*. It is possible that some of these projects may be re-activated in the future.

A HOUSE DIVIDED—Universal—Released December, 1931

Starring: Walter Huston
Directed by William Wyler
Scenarists: John Clymer and Dale Van Every (from a story by Olive
            Edens)
Dialoguer: John Huston

LAW AND ORDER—Universal—Released February, 1932

Starring: Walter Huston
Directed by Edward Cahn
Scenarists: John Huston and Tom Reed (from a story by W. R. Bur-
            nett)

MURDERS IN THE RUE MORGUE—Universal—Released Febru-
                                          ary, 1932

Starring: Bela Lugosi
Directed by Robert Florey
Scenarists: Tom Reed and Dale Every (from a story by Edgar Allan
            Poe)
Dialoguer: John Huston

JEZEBEL—Warner Brothers—Released March, 1938

Starring: Bette Davis, Henry Fonda, George Brent
Directed by William Wyler
Screenplay: John Huston, Clements Ripley and Abem Finkel (from a
            story by Owen Davis)

THE AMAZING DR. CLITTERHOUSE—Warner Brothers—Released
                                          July, 1938

Starring: Edward G. Robinson and Humphrey Bogart
Directed by Anatole Litvak

Screenplay: John Huston and John Wexley (from a story by Barre
    Lyndon)

JUAREZ—Warner Brothers—Released June, 1939

Starring: Paul Muni, Bette Davis, Claude Rains, John Garfield
Directed by William Dieterle
Screenplay: John Huston, Wolfgang Reinhardt and Aeneas MacKenzie
    (from a story by Franz Werfel and Betito Harding)

DR. EHRLICH'S MAGIC BULLET—Warner Brothers—Released
March, 1940

Starring: Edward G. Robinson
Directed by William Dieterle
Screenplay: John Huston, Heinz Herald and Norman Burnside

A PASSENGER TO BALI—(a 3-act play)—March 14–16, 1940

Starring: Walter Huston   At Ethel Barrymore Theater,
Directed by John Huston   New York
Produced by Montgomery Ford
Playwright: Ellis St. Joseph

HIGH SIERRA—Warner Brothers—Released January, 1941

Starring: Humphrey Bogart, Ida Lupino
Directed by Raoul Walsh
Screenplay: John Huston and W. R. Burnett (from the novel by Bur-
    nett)

SERGEANT YORK—Warner Brothers—Released September, 1941

Starring: Gary Cooper, Joan Leslie
Directed by Howard Hawks
Screenplay: John Huston, Howard Koch, Abem Finkel and Harry
    Chandlee (from material on York's life)

THE MALTESE FALCON—Warner Brothers—Released October, 1941

Starring: Humphrey Bogart, Mary Astor, Sydney Greenstreet, Peter
    Lorre, Elisha Cook
Directed by John Huston
Produced by Hal B. Wallis
Screenplay: John Huston (from the novel by Dashiell Hammett)
Photography: Arthur Edeson
Estimated cost: $300,000
Running Time: 100 minutes

IN TIME TO COME—(A play: Prologue and seven scenes)—Dec. 28, 1941–Jan. 31, 1942

Starring: Richard Gaines   At the Mansfield Theater,
Directed by Otto Preminger   New York
Produced by Otto Preminger
Playwrights: John Huston and Howard Koch

IN THIS OUR LIFE—Warner Brothers—Released May, 1942

Starring: Bette Davis, Olivia de Havilland, George Brent, Dennis Mor-
        gan, Charles Coburn
Directed by John Huston
Produced by Hal P. Wallis
Screenplay: Howard Koch (from the novel by Ellen Glasgow)
Photography: Ernest Haller
Estimated cost: Unknown
Running Time: 97 minutes

ACROSS THE PACIFIC—Warner Brothers—Released September, 1942

Starring: Humphrey Bogart, Mary Astor, Sydney Greenstreet
Directed by John Huston
Produced by Jerry Wald and Jack Saper
Screenplay: Richard Macaulay (from *Aloha Means Goodbye* by Robert
        Carson)
Photography: Arthur Edeson
Estimated cost: Unknown
Running time: 97 minutes

REPORT FROM THE ALEUTIANS—(A documentary)—Released
                              by the U.S. Signal Corps in
                              August, 1943

Narration spoken by Walter Huston
Written and directed by Captain John Huston
Running time: 47 minutes

SAN PIETRO—(A documentary)—(Also called THE BATTLE OF
            SAN PIETRO) Released by the U.S. Army Pictorial
            Service in April, 1945

Narration spoken by Major John Huston
Written and directed by Major John Huston
Running time: 32 minutes

LET THERE BE LIGHT—(A documentary)—Restricted: Never officially released. Produced in 1946 for the U.S. Army

Narration spoken by Walter Huston
Directed by John Huston
Running time: not given

THREE STRANGERS—Warner Brothers—Released February, 1946

Starring: Geraldine Fitzgerald, Sydney Greenstreet, Peter Lorre
Directed by Jean Negulesco
Produced by Wolfgang Reinhardt
Screenplay: John Huston and Howard Koch

NO EXIT—(1-act play) November 26–December 21, 1946 at the Biltmore Theater, New York

Starring: Claude Dauphin, Annabella, Ruth Ford
Directed by John Huston
Produced by Herman Levin and Oliver Smith
Playwright: Jean-Paul Sartre (as adapted by Paul Bowles)

THE TREASURE OF THE SIERRA MADRE—Warner Brothers—Released January, 1948

Starring: Humphrey Bogart, Walter Huston, Tim Holt, Alfonso Bedoya, Bruce Bennett
Directed by John Huston
Produced by Henry Blanke
Screenplay: John Huston (from the novel by B. Traven)
Photography: Ted McCord
Estimated cost: $2,800,000
Running time: 126 minutes

KEY LARGO—Warner Brothers—Released July, 1948

Starring: Humphrey Bogart, Lauren Bacall, Edward G. Robinson, Lionel Barrymore, Claire Trevor
Directed by John Huston
Produced by Jerry Wald
Screenplay: John Huston and Richard Brooks (from the play by Maxwell Anderson)
Photography: Karl Freund
Estimated cost: Unknown
Running time: 101 minutes

WE WERE STRANGERS—Columbia-Horizon—Released May, 1949

Starring: John Garfield, Jennifer Jones, Gilbert Roland, Pedro Armen-
    dariz
Directed by John Huston
Produced by "S. P. Eagle" (Sam Spiegel)
Screenplay: John Huston and Peter Viertel (from a segment in *Rough
    Sketch* by Robert Sylvester)
Photography: Russell Metty
Estimated cost: Over $900,000
Running time: 106 minutes

THE ASPHALT JUNGLE—M-G-M—Released June, 1950

Starring: Sterling Hayden, Jean Hagen, Louis Calhern, Sam Jaffe, Mari-
    lyn Monroe
Directed by John Huston
Produced by Arthur Hornblow, Jr.
Screenplay: John Huston and Ben Maddow (from the novel by W. R.
    Burnett)
Photography: Harold Rosson
Estimated cost: Unknown
Running time: 112 minutes

THE RED BADGE OF COURAGE—M-G-M—Released September
                                1951

Starring: Audie Murphy, Bill Mauldin, John Dierkes, Royal Dano,
    Arthur Hunnicutt, Andy Devine
Directed by John Huston
Produced by Gottfried Reinhardt
Screenplay: John Huston (from the novel by Stephen Crane)
Photography: Harold Rosson
Estimated cost: $1,640,000
Running time: 69 minutes

THE AFRICAN QUEEN—United Artists-Horizon-Romulus—Released
                                January, 1952

Starring: Humphrey Bogart, Katherine Hepburn, Robert Morley
Directed by John Huston
Produced by "S. P. Eagle" (Sam Spiegel)
Screenplay: John Huston and James Agee (from the novel by C. S.
    Forester)

Photography: Jack Cardiff
Estimated cost: Unknown
Running time: 106 minutes

MOULIN ROUGE—United Artists-Romulus—Released January, 1953
Starring: Jose Ferrer, Colette Marchand, Zsa Zsa Gabor, Suzanne Flon
Directed by John Huston
Produced by John Huston for Romulus Films
Screenplay: Anthony Veiller (from the novel by Pierre LaMure)
Photography: Oswald Morris
Estimated cost: $1,500,000
Running time: 123 minutes

BEAT THE DEVIL—United Artists-Santana-Romulus—Released March,
                    1954
Starring: Humphrey Bogart, Jennifer Jones, Gina Lollobrigida, Robert
        Morley, Peter Lorre
Directed by John Huston
Produced by John Huston (in association with Humphrey Bogart)
Screenplay: John Huston and Truman Capote (from the novel by James
        Helvick)
Photography: Oswald Morris; Fred Francis
Estimated cost: over $1,000,000
Running time: 92 minutes

MOBY DICK—Warner Brothers—Released June, 1956
Starring: Gregory Peck, Richard Basehart, Leo Genn, Orson Welles
Directed by John Huston
Produced by John Huston
Screenplay: John Huston and Ray Bradbury (from the novel by Herman
        Melville)
Photography: Oswald Morris
Estimated cost: $4,500,000
Running time: 116 minutes

HEAVEN KNOWS, MR. ALLISON—20th Century-Fox—Released
                            March, 1957
Starring: Robert Mitchum and Deborah Kerr
Directed by John Huston
Produced by Buddy Adler and Eugene Frenke

Screenplay: John Huston and John Lee Mahin (from the novel by Charles Shaw)
Photography: Oswald Morris
Estimated cost: $3,000,000
Running time: 107 minutes

THE BARBARIAN AND THE GEISHA—20th Century-Fox—Released October, 1958
Starring: John Wayne, Sam Jaffe, Eiko Ando, So Yamayura
Directed by John Huston
Produced by Eugene Frenke
Screenplay: Charles Grayson (from a story by Ellis St. Joseph)
Photography: Charles G. Clarke
Estimated cost: $3,500,000
Running time: 105 minutes

THE ROOTS OF HEAVEN—20th Century-Fox—Released December, 1958
Starring: Errol Flynn, Trevor Howard, Juliette Greco, Eddie Albert, Paul Lukas, Orson Welles
Directed by John Huston
Produced by Darryl F. Zanuck
Screenplay: Romain Gary and Patrick Leigh-Fermor (from the novel by Gary)
Photography: Oswald Morris
Estimated cost: $4,500,000
Running time: 131 minutes

THE UNFORGIVEN—United Artists—Released April, 1960
Starring: Burt Lancaster, Audrey Hepburn, Audie Murphy, Charles Bickford, Lillian Gish, John Saxon, Joseph Wiseman.
Directed by John Huston
Produced by James Hill
Screenplay: Ben Maddow (from a novel by Alan LeMay)
Photography: Franz Planer
Estimated cost: Over $5,000,000
Running time: 125 minutes

THE MISFITS—United Artists—Released February, 1961
Starring: Clark Gable, Marilyn Monroe, Montgomery Clift, Thelma Ritter, Eli Wallach

Directed by John Huston
Produced by Frank Taylor
Screenplay: Arthur Miller (based on his short story)
Photography: Russell Metty
Estimated cost: $4,000,000

Running time: 124 minutes

FREUD (also called THE SECRET PASSION)—Universal—Released
      January, 1963

Starring: Montgomery Clift, Susannah York, Larry Parks, Susan Kohner
Directed by John Huston
Produced by Wolfgang Reinhardt
Screenplay: Charles Kaufman and Wolfgang Reinhardt
Photography: Douglas Slocombe
Estimated cost: Unknown

Running time: 139 minutes

THE LIST OF ADRIAN MESSENGER—Universal—Released
      August, 1963

Starring: Kirk Douglas, George C. Scott, Dana Wynter, Herbert Mar-
      shall (with Tony Curtis, Robert Mitchum, Frank Sinatra,
      Burt Lancaster)
Directed by John Huston
Produced by Edward Lewis
Screenplay: Anthony Veiller (from the novel by Philip MacDonald)
Photography: Joseph MacDonald
Estimated cost: $3,000,000

Running time: 98 minutes

THE CARDINAL—Columbia—Released December, 1963

Starring: Tom Tryon, Romy Schneider, John Saxon, Carol Lynley, Raf
      Vallone, Burgess Meredith and John Huston as Glennon
Directed by Otto Preminger
Produced by Otto Preminger
Screenplay: Robert Dozier (from the novel by Henry Morton Robinson)

THE NIGHT OF THE IGUANA—M-G-M/Seven Arts—Released
      July, 1964

Starring: Richard Burton, Ava Gardner, Deborah Kerr, Sue Lyon, Gray-
      son Hall
Directed by John Huston
Produced by Ray Stark

Screenplay: John Huston and Anthony Veiller (from the play by
            Tennessee Williams)
Photography: Gabriel Figueroa
Estimated cost: $3,000,000
Running time: 118 minutes

THE BIBLE—Dino De Laurentiis—To be released in 1965

Starring: Peter O'Toole, George C. Scott, Richard Harris, Ava Gardner,
          Stephen Boyd and John Huston as Noah
Directed by John Huston
Produced by Dino De Laurentiis
Screenplay: Christopher Fry
Photography: Giuseppe Rotunno
Estimated cost: $15,000,000

NOTE: Six of Huston's films have grossed four million or over in U.S.-
      Canadian outlets, as follows:
            MOBY DICK—$5,200,000
            MOULIN ROUGE—$5,000,000
            HEAVEN KNOWS, MR. ALLISON—$4,200,000
            THE AFRICAN QUEEN—$4,100,000
            THE MISFITS—$4,100,000
            THE NIGHT OF THE IGUANA—$4,000,000

A HUSTON BIBLIOGRAPHY

NOTE: The titles listed here include most, but not all, of the published material on John Huston which has been put between covers. As far as possible, all work *by* Huston in book form is also listed. Each section is arranged by year of publication.

PLAYS, SCREENPLAYS and FICTION

Huston, John, *Frankie and Johnny*, Boni, 1930
(This is Huston's only book, and is a play in three scenes, with a song listing, illustrated by Covarrubias.)

Mantle, Burns (Editor), *The Best Plays of 1941–1942*, Dodd, Mead & Co., 1942
(This anthology contains an abridged, edited text of *In Time to Come*, by Howard Koch and John Huston.)

Gassner, John and Nichols, Dudley (Editors), *Twenty Best Film Plays*, Crown Publishers, Inc., 1943. (This collection contains the complete text of the screenplay, *Juarez*, by John Huston, Wolfgang Reinhardt and Aeneas MacKenzie.)

Grayson, Charles (Editor), *New Stories for Men*, Garden City Publishing Co., 1943.
(This anthology of short fiction contains *Fool*, by John Huston.)

Viertel, Peter, *White Hunter, Black Heart*, Doubleday and Co., Inc., 1953
(This novel centers around a character named "John Wilson," for which Huston served as the basis. It is a well-known, much-discussed volume which brings Huston vividly to life in a fictional guise.)

Busch, Niven, *The Actor*, Simon and Schuster, Inc., 1955
(This novel includes a character named "Harold Heston" for which Huston served as the basis.)

Hamblett, Charles, *The Crazy Kill*, Sidgwick and Jackson, Ltd., 1956
(This novel deals—in semi-fictional form—with the filming of *Moby Dick*. Introduction by Huston. Published in England.)

Agee, James, *Agee on Film: Volume 2*, McDowell, Obolensky, Inc., 1960
(This collection of Agee's screenplays contains a Foreword by John Huston.)

Hughes, Robert (Editor), *Film: Book 2*, Grove Press, Inc., 1962.
(This anthology has the complete text of Huston's *Let There Be Light*— as well as an interview with him.)

Bradbury, Ray, *The Anthem Sprinters*, The Dial Press, Inc., 1963
(This collection of short Irish plays is dedicated to Huston, and contains comment by the author on *Moby Dick*.)

BIOGRAPHIES and AUTOBIOGRAPHIES

Kilbracken, John, *Living Like a Lord*, Houghton Mifflin Co., 1956
(Contains two chapters dealing with Huston and *Moby Dick*.)

Pearson, Billy (with Stephen Longstreet), *Never Look Back*, Simon and Schuster, Inc., 1958 (Pearson's career, with an Introduction by John Huston, plus several chapters involving him.)

Flynn, Errol, *My Wicked, Wicked Ways*, G. P. Putnam's Sons, 1959
(Contains data on *The Roots of Heaven*.)

Frank, Gerold, *Zsa Zsa-My Story*, World Book Co., 1960
(Contains a passage involving Gabor and *Moulin Rouge*.)

Zolotow, Maurice, *Marilyn Monroe*, Harcourt Brace and Co., 1960
(Contains a brief passage on how Monroe was hired by Huston for *The Asphalt Jungle*.)

Davis, Bette, *The Lonely Life,* G. P. Putnam's Sons, 1962
(Contains brief notes on how Davis worked with Huston.)

Hayden, Sterling, *Wanderer,* Alfred A. Knopf, Inc., 1963 (Contains a brief passage on how Hayden was hired by Huston for *The Asphalt Jungle.*)

CRITICISM, ANTHOLOGIES, REPORTAGE

Ross, Lillian, *Picture,* Rinehart and Co., 1952
(Contains the five *New Yorker* articles written on the making of *The Red Badge of Courage.* Excellent job.)

Rotha, Paul, *Documentary Film,* Faber and Faber, Ltd., 1952
(This third edition of the British book contains data on Huston's wartime documentaries.)

Crowther, Bosley, *The Lion's Share,* E. P. Dutton, 1957
(Contains data on Huston at M-G-M.)

Knight, Arthur, *The Liveliest Art,* The Macmillan Co., 1957
(Check the index for data on Huston.)

Agee, James, *Agee on Film,* McDowell, Obolensky, Inc., 1958
(Contains criticism on a number of Huston films, plus Agee's *Life* profile on him.)

Goodman, Ezra, *The Fifty-Year Decline and Fall of Hollywood,* Simon and Schuster, Inc., 1961.
(Contains data on Huston, plus a short profile of him.)

Alpert, Hollis, *The Dreams and the Dreamers,* The Macmillan Co., 1962
(Contains a short profile on Huston.)

Rivkin, Allen with Kerr, Laura (Editors), *Hello, Hollywood!,* Doubleday and Co., Inc., 1962.
(Contains data by and about Huston.)

Goode, James, *The Story of the Misfits,* Bobbs-Merrill Co., 1963
(A day-by-day report on the making of the film.)